Afterglow of Christ's Resurrection

the radiance over New Testament literature

by Alger M. Fitch, Jr.

A Division of Standard Publishing
Cincinnati, Ohio
40030

ISBN: 0-87239-055-1

Library of Congress Catalog Card Number: 75-14692

preface

I supposed I knew my Bible,
   Reading piecemeal hit or miss.
Now a bit of John or Matthew,
   Now a snatch from Genesis;
Certain chapters of Isaiah,
   Certain Psalms, the Twenty-third,
Twelfth of Romans, first of Proverbs—
   Yes, I thought I knew the Word!
But I found that thorough reading
   Was a different thing to do,
And the way was unfamiliar
   When I read the Bible through.

You who love to play at Bible,
   Dip and dabble here and there,
Just before you kneel aweary,
   Yawning through a hurried prayer;
You who treat the crown of writings
   As you treat no other book—
Just a paragraph disjointed,
   Just a crude, impatient look—
Why not try a thorough reading?
   Try a broad and steady view.
You will kneel in very rapture,
   When you read the Bible through.[1]

The poet is right. A thorough reading of the Bible is an "enrapturing" experience. We invite you in this book to survey afresh the entire New Testament. We want you to see each part in perspective, and to view every portion in relation to the whole. We will be taking, in order, the four sections of the New Testament: the four Gospels; the book of Acts; all the epistles; and finally, the book of Revelation. After an overview of the four types of literature in the New Testament, we expect that each Scripture portion will take on more meaning to you.

---

[1]Amos R. Wells, "Read the Bible Through" in *The Speaker's Treasury of 400 Quotable Poems* (Grand Rapids, Michigan: Zondervan Publishing House, 1963), p. 11.

As we stroll through the familiar territory of sacred Scripture, we will look for the ideas suggested by the headings over each part of this present volume. Part One: What is "the gospel in the *Gospels*"? Part Two: What are "the acts of the apostles in the *Acts of the Apostles*"? Here we will not seek to underscore the acts of elders, deacons, worshipers, or common disciples, but will direct attention to the acts of the apostles after whom the Bible book has been named. Next, in Part Three, we will seek to comprehend "the pastoring in the *Pastorals*." This chapter title does not limit the inquiry to 1 and 2 Timothy and Titus, to which the term "pastoral" is usually applied, but rather recognizes that all of the epistles were written out of pastoral concern. Then, in Part Four, we will look for the specific "revelation" presented by John "in the book of *Revelation*." Throughout this study we shall see that the testimony coming out of all four literary types of the New Covenant Scriptures is the witness to Jesus' resurrection.

The title given to the present volume reflects this last statement. The New Testament, both in its totality and in its individual sections, radiates the resurrection of the Lord. That glorious truth glistens on every page of the twenty-seven books in our New Testament.

"The gospel in the *Gospels*" is the gospel of Jesus once crucified, but now risen. "The acts of the apostles in the *Acts of the Apostles*" are their acts of witnessing to the risen Lord. "The pastoring in the *Pastorals*" is the continuance of the resurrected Christ's shepherding care of His people through His people. "The revelation in the *Revelation*" is that of the risen and ascended Christ conquering the world. In other words, the testimony of the Testament in all its parts is to the fact that He who died for our sins has risen from the grave "according to the Scriptures."

Afterglow of Christ's Resurrection: The Radiance over New Testament Literature.

—The Author

table of contents

Part One: The Gospel in the *Gospels* 7

  1 / the gospel 7
  2 / the gospels 11
  3 / the joyful sound 15
  4 / mark's good news 19
  5 / matthew's good news 23
  6 / luke's good news 29
  7 / john's good news 35

**Part Two: The Acts of the Apostles
         in the *Acts of the Apostles*** 41

  8 / acts 41
  9 / the leading characters 45
  10 / the happy endings 55
  11 / the opening scenes 61
  12 / the dramatic acts 67

Part Three: The Pastoring in the *Pastorals* 71

  13 / pastorals 71
  14 / pastoral in heart 75
  15 / pastoral in nature 83
  16 / pastoral in need 95

Part Four: The Revelation in the *Revelation* 99

  17 / revelation 99
  18 / the church at war 105
  19 / the church at work 111
  20 / the church at worship 123

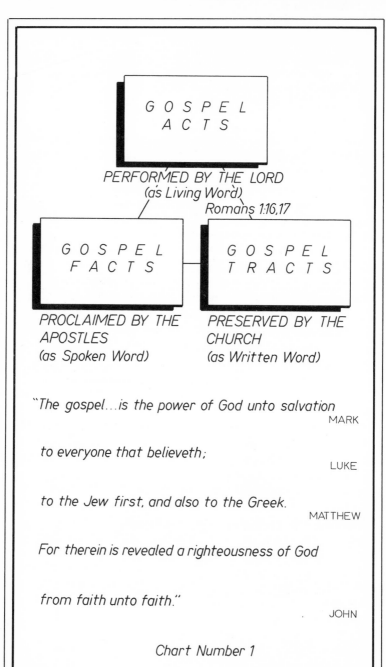

GOSPEL
ACTS

PERFORMED BY THE LORD
(as Living Word)
Romans 1:16,17

GOSPEL
FACTS

GOSPEL
TRACTS

PROCLAIMED BY THE
APOSTLES
(as Spoken Word)

PRESERVED BY THE
CHURCH
(as Written Word)

"The gospel...is the power of God unto salvation
MARK

to everyone that believeth;
LUKE

to the Jew first, and also to the Greek.
MATTHEW

For therein is revealed a righteousness of God

from faith unto faith."
JOHN

Chart Number 1

1 / the gospel

Open your Bible to the literary *genre* that is placed at the front of your New Testament—the Gospels. They were not the first books of the New Testament to be written. They are placed first, however, since only individuals interested in the person of Jesus revealed there would have an interest in reading any of the literature written to and by His followers. Maybe you will want temporarily to put a bookmark at the opening chapter of each story of Christ—those written by Matthew, Mark, Luke, and John.

There is a multiple meaning in the word GOSPEL. Each sense should be clarified in Chart #1. Catch the significance in the chronological order. First, there was the event of Christ's coming, His death, His burial, His resurrection, His ascension on high. These were GOSPEL ACTS. They happened in history long before we ever had any written part of our New Testament. Shortly after the final gospel event in Christ's earthly life, we find the apostles going everywhere, as eyewitnesses of these events. They declared these GOSPEL FACTS along with accompanying gospel promises and gospel commands.

Fortunately for us today, the church has preserved, in written form, some Gospel accounts that have come down to us (see Luke 1:1-4). These now constitute the first part of our New Testament. So we move historically from GOSPEL ACTS to the GOSPEL FACTS to the GOSPEL TRACTS. Or, put another way, after the "performance" by the Lord, we have the "proclamation" by the apostles and finally the "preservation" of their witness by the church. Thus the Word of God is first the *living Word,* Christ come into history. Then it became the *spoken word,* the oral preaching by which faith in Christ was produced (Romans 10:17). Only lastly did it become the preserved or *written Word* called Holy Scripture.

Right in the center of Chart #1 you see the Scripture reference, Romans 1:16, 17. These verses talk about the good news of the gospel:

> The Gospel . . . is the power of God unto salvation to every one that believeth; to the Jew first, and also to the Greek. For therein is revealed a righteousness of God from faith unto faith: as it is written, But the righteous shall live by faith.[1]

This passage does not list gospel facts such as you find recorded in 1 Corinthians 15:1-4 or 1 Timothy 3:16. It is rather a statement about the gospel's consequence. But, for our purposes, it is interesting to notice that all four of the Gospel writers confirm Paul's entire statement in Romans. And each author has emphasized above the other penman one special phase of that truth. For instance, the theme of *Mark,* the first written Gospel, is "the gospel is the power of God unto salvation." Mark proclaimed that the good news was evident in the dramatic power of Jesus Christ to make whole (i.e. to make complete, to save, to rescue). The Gospel of Mark, after illustrating this healing power with one miracle after another, ends with the commission in 16:15, 16: "Go ye into all the world, and preach the gospel to the whole creation. He that believeth and is baptized shall be saved." The word "saved," or "made whole," is the same word used to describe what Christ did in every healing. The testimony of Mark is to the power of God, to the miracles of God, to the ability of God to do the impossible even in your life. So, while Jesus' saving power is to some degree the theme in all four Gospel documents before us, it is especially the message of Mark.

The next phrase of Romans 1:16 "to every one that believeth," is the truth that impressed Luke. He was a Gentile. He was not of the twelve tribes but was an outsider as far as God's Covenant was concerned. Rejoicing that Christianity included "the likes of him," Luke wrote his volume to herald the wonder that God's gospel was not exclusively for the Jews. Indeed, Christ came to the Jew first. But Jesus' blessings were to anyone and everyone who would believe.

When Matthew picked up his pen, he not only reaffirmed what Mark had recorded, and shouted agreement with what Luke believed, he stressed firmly that the divine message was "to the Jew first," while most certainly "also to the Greek." In your previous reading of Matthew you already have noticed

---

[1] All Scriptures are from the *American Standard Version.*

that Jesus was born the King of the Jews. Yet, at the same time, people from the distant Orient came to give him gifts. The same awareness that the long-awaited Jewish Messiah was to bless all people, continues through the final chapter of Matthew's account. There Jesus' final declaration requests His followers to "make disciples of all the nations" (Matthew 28:19), for they too are included in God's plans as well as the Jew. It may be said then, that the synoptic Gospels (Matthew, Mark, and Luke) give special emphasis to the truth of the first portion of Romans 1:16, 17.

John, who wrote last of all the apostles, the others being dead, declared unto us how each disciple's faith developed. It was "from faith unto faith" (Romans 1:17). It was from initial faith like that expressed by Nathanael in the words, "thou art King of Israel" (John 1:49), to even greater faith like that shown by prostrate Thomas in his cry, "My Lord and my God" (John 20:28). As John's Gospel described it, the disciples' convictions blossomed from a nucleus faith to an overwhelming faith. He told us in his purpose-verses of John 20:30, 31 that these deeds of Jesus were written for the same reason that they earlier were told. The purpose of the telling was so men could believe and, coming to faith, could have life in His name.

We have tried to make clear that all the TRACTS (the written documents) are based on the FACTS that had been preached so many years before by oral proclamation. Those heralded FACTS dealt with the ACTS of God in our sphere of time and space. With our terms defined, we are now ready to move to the four Gospels themselves and review once again data such as when they were written and what they emphasize.

Matthew

Mark

GOSPELS

John

Luke

Chart Number 2

2 / the gospels

An understanding of some background material on Matthew, Mark, Luke, and John will equip us in our search for the gospel in the Gospels.

As to dates and places of writing for these books, we assert first that Mark was the earliest Gospel of the four. It was finalized shortly after A.D. 64, about the time of the death of Peter. Burnett Hillman Streeter[1] dates Matthew and Luke around A.D. 80 or 85 and the Gospel of John maybe as late as A.D. 95. We may accept much earlier dates than these, as long as we allow for the order of Mark first and John last. I believe Matthew to have been written from Antioch; Mark, from Rome; Luke, from Corinth; and John, from the city of Ephesus.

The four symbols (the living creatures of Revelation 4:6, 7 and Ezekiel 1:10 and 10:14) usually given in art to picture these four Gospels have been variously assigned to different sources. These symbols are arranged logically to my mind in this order: For Matthew, the "lion" is a good image because his Gospel emphasizes Christ as King. For Mark, the "ox" or "calf" is fitting because his work illustrates Christ's service and His sacrifice. The "face of a man" is fitting for Luke's narrative for it pictures the humanity and compassion of Jesus Christ. The "eagle," which soars high above in the heavens, symbolizes the transcendence of John's spiritual Gospel. (See Chart #2.)

The perspective of writing, then, for Matthew is the past. The perspective for Mark is the present—the now. The perspective for Luke is history extending on into the future. The perspective for John is all eternity. Keep in mind that the key word of each Gospel relates to the author's perspective. In Matthew the key word is "fulfilled," because that term looks back to the past and to all the promises, hopes, and dreams of Old Testament times. Why Matthew appears as the first book

---

[1]*The Four Gospels: A Study of Origins* (London: Macmillan and Co., Ltd., 1956).

in your New Testament is not that it was written first, as we have already said. Rather, of all the Gospel's Matthew's is the most closely related to the Old Testament. Nineteen of its ancient books are used by him. Sixty-five times he makes reference to, or draws out, prophecies from the Old Covenant Scriptures. Thirteen times a prediction about the Messiah is placed alongside its fulfillment in the life of Jesus with the refrain, "this happened that it might be fulfilled which was spoken by the prophet." Mark, writing for the Romans, accents the power of God for today. Hence, the key word of Mark is "straightway" or "immediately." Mark wanted his contemporaries to know that the power from Heaven is available "now." He makes this evident in relating the activities of the never-tiring Jesus. The key word of Luke is "compassion" or "sympathy." The fact that God ever cares is the truth made so clear in his record of Jesus' teaching and life. The key word of John is "belief."

The good news, the joyful tidings, the glad message is what God has done for us in the person of His Son. As each writer tells his happy story, his reader is aware that he is hearing a confession of faith—a gospel sermon. He is not reading a detailed biography or a short life of Christ, but what Willi Marxen[2] calls *predict* (preaching, proclamation). The authors are not biographers. They are evangelists. And we are ready to hear their testimony. (See Chart #3.)

---

[2] Professor of Protestant Theology, Westfalische Wilhelms-Universitat Munster.

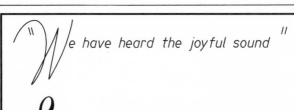
"We have heard the joyful sound"

JESUS SAVES

MARK

JESUS IS SOVEREIGN

MATTHEW

JESUS SEEKS

LUKE

JESUS SATISFIES

JOHN

Chart Number 3

3 / the joyful sound

The sermons that you read in brief form in the book of Acts are in expanded form in our written Gospels. That is what these books are. They are sermons telling why their authors believe that Jesus is the Christ, the Son of the Living God. The written Gospels are passion and resurrection testimonies with enough introduction that it will be evident who this Jesus is who died for sins and rose again.

While the authors believe the same gospel and relate similar facts in their sermons, they use different phrases, terms, and emphases. The hearing of each testimony makes the worshiper's heart to hear and then to sing something like this: "We have heard *the joyful sound:* JESUS SAVES!" That is, He heals, He rescues, He makes whole again. This is the recurring refrain of Mark. Like another stanza to the same hymn is Matthew's chant of *the joyful sound,* JESUS IS SOVEREIGN. He is King of Kings and Lord of Lords. Luke adds an additional verse to the familiar air. From this we hear the happy lilt that JESUS SEEKS. He seeks to save that which is lost. John says, JESUS SATISFIES. His Gospel brings to crescendo the faith in each of the other Gospels. He pulls out all the stops in his emphasis on Christ's true humanity and deity. His is the grand melody that the God-man completely "satisfies" every need of every person. As He helped a woman at a well who was thirsting for water, Jesus will help others to find in himself the water that brings complete satisfaction in every human situation.

The key verse of each Gospel substantiates these observations. Mark 10:45 reports that Jesus as *Servant-Savior* "came not to be ministered unto, but to minister, and to give his life a ransom for many." Matthew 1:1 asserts that He who is "the son of David" is, of course, "the Son of God" who is going to *reign* over mankind. Note how the opening words of the entire Gospel by Matthew—"the generation of Jesus Christ"—are a deliberate pointer to the Old Testament book of Genesis and its use of the phrase, "the book of the generations of . . ."

(Genesis 5:1, etc.). Luke 19:10 declares that Jesus came "to *seek* and to save that which was lost." Consistent to the emphasis on seeking, it is in Luke's Gospel that you find such a chapter as Luke 15 about a father seeking for a returning son, a shepherd seeking for a lost sheep, and a lady sweeping her house seeking for a lost coin. The heart of the heavenly Father is seeking everyone outside the fold. John 20:30, 31 echoes the evangelistic concern of the church and promises the "life" in Jesus' name that *satisfies* our innermost hungers:

> Many other signs therefore did Jesus in the presence of the disciples, which are not written in this book: but these are written, that ye may believe that Jesus is the Christ, the Son of God; and that believing ye may have life in his name.

It has been suggested that the first three Evangelist's testimonies, those termed the synoptic Gospels, present the good confession that Jesus is the Christ, while the last Gospel completes this well-begun creed with the truth that this Christ is the Son of God. *Messiah* (Hebrew) and *Christ* (Greek) mean the anointed one, implying to those with an Old Testament background that God's anointed would be prophet, priest, and king. The kingship of Jesus is Matthew's topic. The priesthood of Jesus and His sacrifice is Mark's theme. Jesus, the prophet who speaks out the heavenly message to all humanity, is Luke's subject matter. John, from his opening line, is underscoring words that call Jesus "God" and is detailing signs and sayings that show the incarnate Jesus (the Word made flesh) to be Immanuel—God with us.

*M*ark's good news: JESUS CHRIST IS SAVIOR

JESUS

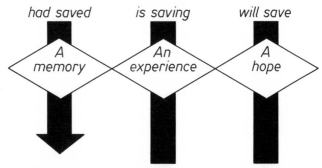

had saved   is saving   will save

A memory   An experience   A hope

MARK'S EXAMPLES from Christ's ministry

A.D. 26-30

MARK'S EXPERIENCE in Peter's and
Paul's ministry

A.D. 30-64

MARK'S EXPECTATIONS for the
Church's ministry ❓
A.D. 64-2000

Chart Number 4

4 / mark's good news

Now, let us glance again at each Gospel account one at a time, starting with Mark. (See Chart #4.) The good news that JESUS CHRIST IS SAVIOR is the theme of this shortest Gospel.

Mark has not written, nor meant to imply, that Jesus *had saved* and that that saving power was only a thing of bygone days. He has added the even more marvelous wonder that the same Jesus who had saved *is saving* still. The events he recorded in Jesus' life from the baptism of John up to the climactic happenings of A.D. 30 have now long been past. Some thirty-four years later, when Mark finalized his Gospel, he knew the same Christ to be saving others daily before his very eyes. Also, we may infer, he anticipated the whole of human history and changed the verb of salvation he has used from *had saved* (past tense) to *is saving* (present tense) and to *will save* (future tense). Note that the Gospel of Mark ends with a Great Commission by this resurrected Christ. Especially observe that it is anticipated that evangelization will continue on until the end of time: "He that believeth and is baptized *shall be* saved" (Mark 16:16).

As Mark prepared to write, he had a happy "Memory" of the crucifixion-resurrection event which had taken place in Jerusalem several years before. But in Rome now (after the "big fisherman," Peter, had been silenced through martyrdom in the persecution of Nero), Mark is recalling his personal and more recent "Experience." He had ministered with Paul in the first missionary journey and later with Peter as his interpreter. But, before Mark laid aside his writing implement, he moved from the past memory of Christ's ministry, through his present experience in Peter's and Paul's ministry, to his future "Hope" and expectation for the church's ministry. All the world and every creature in any age yet to come was to know that, while the world stands, what the Lord *had done* and *is doing,* He *will* continue to *do.* Jesus *had saved, is saving,* and *will* continue to *save.*

Mark's Examples

Mark's EXAMPLES from Christ's ministry are drawn from the earlier years, A.D. 26-30. Jesus was then ministering in the flesh from His baptism in the waters of the Jordan up to His baptism of suffering on the cross at Jerusalem. In these samples we observe that Jesus did many mighty works that were signs pointing to who He then was and still is.

Each miracle recorded in this Gospel not only stands as a manifestation of the power of God but as a revelation of the love of God. It could not be considered good news, if God were able to help us but did not care about us. It would not even be good news if God cared, but our problems were too great for Him to handle. It is the combination of His power and His love that is such good news.

Mark had heard Peter and Paul tell of many instances from the life of Jesus where He would heal a leper, or say to a dead man, "Arise!" or order a bent man, "Stand Straight!" So Mark simply picks out a sample here or a sample there to show the variety of sicknesses or problems that Jesus could handle. Why? So that whatever his reader's dilemma, he will know Christ can overcome that as well. Among the examples given is that of a woman with the issue of blood. Another is the case of a leprous man. Although there were many women helped or lepers healed, a single instance is enough to let the reader know that in whatever predicament he finds himself, the same Christ is ready, able, and willing to help him. This is the aim of each of Mark's EXAMPLES brought into this little testimony of sixteen chapters.

Mark's Experience

Now I want your eye to move on Chart #4 from the line on Mark's EXAMPLES to the line on Mark's EXPERIENCE. This refers to our writer's participation in ministries with Peter and Paul. According to early church-history records by Eusebius, Papias is said to have called Mark the "interpreter" of Peter. This may mean that through his Gospel, Mark had passed on to the church what he so often had heard this great apostle preach. This tradition goes way back and is very likely the case. If it is, Mark has written for us what many times Peter had proclaimed as an eyewitness and minister of the Word. It is true that Mark is not an apostle. His writing, however, is considered apostolic testimony, because it is Mark's recording of what he has heard the apostles preach. While Mark ministered with Peter, and when he traveled with Paul, he saw that the saving power of God was not taken from the earth at Christ's ascension into Heaven. The Gospels record only what Jesus "began to do and to teach." This is declared by Luke in Acts 1:1. This phrasing affirms that the Lord of the church was yet at the work of man's salvation. He was still teaching and acting through these men He had chosen and qualified with miracle power.

Mark's Expectations

As we further peruse this Gospel written in Rome, we are reminded of Mark's EXAMPLES from Christ's ministry. We are aware of Mark's EXPERIENCE in Peter's and Paul's ministry. We also are caught up with Mark's EXPECTATIONS for the church's ministry. This is expected to last through all time that yet may pass, from Peter's death in A.D. 64 until that time when Jesus Christ shall come again.

Do you want to be saved from the stain of sin? from the pain of sin? from the strain of sin? Do you want to be saved from its guilt? from its power? from its penalty? When you read this inspired record of Mark, you find out that Jesus not only "had saved," but "is saving," and "will continue to save." All you have to do is what the "old, old story" states was done by Christ's contemporaries. They trusted in Him. They followed Him. If you will trust in Him and go where He leads, you will find Him adequate for your particular need. This is the good news that sounds forth from the Gospel of Mark. JESUS SAVES!

Matthew's good news: Jesus Christ is King

THE

R	IGORS	*of His Reign (5-7)*
E	MISSARIES	*of His Reign (10)*
I	LLUSTRATIONS	*of His Reign (13)*
G	REATNESS	*of His Reign (18)*
N	EGLECT	*of His Reign (23-25)*

Chart Number 5

5 / matthew's good news

How is this Christian hope expressed in the message of Matthew? Here the good news is that Jesus is sovereign, that JESUS CHRIST IS KING. John the Baptist had been predicting the kingdom of Heaven to be at hand. This had become the message of Jesus, then the message of the twelve, and still later the message of the seventy. By the time our aged apostle wrote his testimony from Antioch, Jesus had been "reigning" from His throne at God's right hand for over thirty years.

One difference between Mark's Gospel and Matthew's Gospel is that whereas Mark gives you mainly the action of Jesus, Matthew gives you (in addition to that action) the teaching of the KING. Six hundred of Mark's 661 verses basically reappear in Matthew along with Jesus' sayings. These sayings constitute three-fifths of this Gospel. Where Mark is preacher, Matthew is teacher. You would have expected this because Matthew 28:19, 20 concludes Matthew's account. Here the risen Lord is saying that we are to disciple the nations and then to teach the baptized to observe all that Christ has commanded. From the Gospel of Mark we learned little of what Christ had said or commanded. We have gained that knowledge by the further information added by Matthew and others.

Matthew had been a tax collector. He had kept records most of his life. It would appear likely that one reason Christ had called him to be among His apostles was to serve as secretary. Peter acted as chairman or spokesman. Judas served as treasurer. No logic can decry the suggestion that the lot of secretary well could have fallen on Levi (as Edgar J. Goodspeed has argued in his work, *Matthew: Apostle and Martyr*). Thus it might be that, when the Sermon on the Mount was given by the Lord or he related kingdom parables in chapter 13, Matthew recorded these from the time they were spoken. Some think Matthew may not be only the author of the Gospel that now bears his name but the *amanuensis* or secretary who earlier made a copy of the words or teachings. In technical journals this reputed source of Jesus' sayings is called *logia,* the Greek word for saying, or "Q," the first letter in *quelle,* the German word for source. This much is certain, Matthew did go beyond Mark's Gospel by adding some teachings of Jesus. This he has done in five places. The insertion of *didache* (teaching) in five instances is not accidental.[1] It is notable that many old Jewish works, such as Moses' writings, the Psalms of David, and the *Pirke Aboth,* also were divided into five sections.

Matthew is writing the new Pentateuch deliberately to replace the old. Appealing to the Jewish mind, he says that JESUS CHRIST IS KING of Israel. This new Israel, today, is constituted of all people who believe in and follow Jesus. Matthew is asserting that Jesus is the new Moses who has come to deliver the people from a Satanic bondage worse than Pharaoh's. As there were Genesis, Exodus, Leviticus, Numbers, and Deuteronomy in the Old Testament *Torah* given through Moses, the new deliverer has brought to God's new Israel five great teachings. Matthew, perhaps recalling Mount Sinai, says Christ also went up into a mountain (Matthew 5:1). Yet, Jesus did not bring another law with ten commandments—He delivered the gospel of His "kingdom."

Rigor's of His Reign

As a memory aid to your study of Matthew, use the acrostic *R E I G N,* as in Chart #5. In the Sermon on the Mount of chapters 5, 6, and 7 you have the RIGORS of His *reign.* Here Christ reveals that Christianity supercedes the Old Testament. He leaves no doubt that we have moved to higher ground, not lower. To believe that the law of Moses no longer binds the church is not to move into antinomianism and to claim freedom to live an immoral and undisciplined life. The Christian rigor of the teaching is reflected in a phrase of E. Stanley Jones: "The Sermon on the Mount without the Christ of the Mount is a staggering impossibility." In Jesus' hillside homily, which contrasts the new with the old, He said, "Ye have heard that it was said to them of old time, Thou shalt not kill; . . . but *I* say unto you . . . Ye have heard that it was said, Thou shalt not commit adultery: but *I* say unto you, . . ." In every case

---

[1]R. G. V. Trasker early noted this fact and B. W. Bacon built on his discovery.

Jesus made more rigorous demands than did Moses. The proposition of that Sermon on the Mount is, "Your righteousness shall exceed the righteousness of the scribes and Pharisees" (Matthew 5:20). The Pharisees were not basically evil men. They strove more diligently than others to keep the commandments of God. They were the examples from among the Jews. Yet, disciples of Jesus must do better because they follow One who is better than Moses. This truth is in the good news by Matthew that the reign of Christ takes us to a higher mount than even Mount Sinai. It brings us to a heavenly Mount Zion, the city of the living God.

Emissaries of His Reign

In chapter 10 you have instruction concerning the EMISSARIES of His *reign.* What will these twelve ambassadors especially do? When you consider this part of our acrostic remember to ask not only who is speaking, but to whom those promises and assignments are specifically given. In Matthew 10, out of all of His disciples, Christ has called together only twelve. These He has designated "apostles." He is telling them what their peculiar orders will be. He indicates what special powers will be given them as they go out to "heal the sick, raise the dead, cleanse the lepers" (Matthew 10:8). They are assured that they will not have to think ahead of time what they are going to say or how they are going to say it. It will be given them in that hour (verses 19, 20). We are hearing, in this ordination sermon, unique instructions for the twelve ambassadors of Christ. They will "reign" according to another passage from this same book, throughout "the regeneration" period sitting on "twelve thrones, judging the twelve tribes of Israel" (Matthew 19:28).

Illustrations of His Reign

Another place of teaching is chapter 13 where we find the ILLUSTRATIONS of His *reign,* or the parables of the kingdom. These are seven in number, you will remember. Matthew, being a teacher, gives this number as a memory aid just as he uses other such aids throughout his book. Of the many things Jesus said in parable about the kingdom of God, Matthew chooses seven to use here.

Without going into detail regarding the illustrations found in chapter 13, you will recall the beautiful comparison of Jesus' preaching to a sower going forth to sow, and the kingdom of Heaven's growth to a grain of mustard seed developing into a bush to fill the entire earth. You will call to mind Jesus saying that the kingdom of Heaven would spread like leaven, quietly but surely working until the entire lump was leavened. You will remember further how the kingdom of Heaven was to be akin to a treasure accidentally discovered in the field. In that case the person involved was willing to sell anything and everything to make the precious possession his own. Yet again, in an opposite instance from accidental discovery, Jesus added that the kingdom of Heaven would be like a pearl for which a man had been searching. When he found that for which he so long sought, all of his possessions became as nothing compared to this which he had discovered. To these stories are added the parable of the tares and the parable of the net. Matthew has picked out exactly seven. Each window (parable) has let additional light pour into the room of our mind so that we can see more clearly the nature of Christ's kingdom.

Greatness of His Reign

In chapter 18, the theme is the GREATNESS of His *reign.* Here the disciples had been arguing about who would be the greatest in the kingdom of Heaven. Jesus put a child in their midst. He taught them, by this living visual aid, that greatness is in service and humility and teachability.

Neglect of His Reign

Finally, the tragedy of neglect is seen in the "little apocalypse" of the book of Matthew, chapters 23, 24, and 25. In chapter 23 there are seven woes against the Pharisees who had shown neglect. They had rejected their king. This rebuke is justification for the prophesies to follow. In chapter 24 appear the three predictions about coming events, the first of which is the inevitable consequence of the Jewish NEGLECT of His *reign.* First will come the fall of Jerusalem as God rejects the Jewish nation. Then will follow the evangelization of the Gentiles. Lastly will occur the return of Christ. In chapter

25 are found three great illustrations of the need for pre-paredness.

Being acquainted with Mark's story, we know what Jesus did. This record of his doings Matthew has repeated and additionally has interlaced teaching sections. Each of these units of instruction has ended with the brief remark, "When Jesus had finished these words" (Matthew 7:28). The recurring phrase with similar wording found in 11:1, 13:53, 19:1, and 26:1, has made Matthew's literary plan obvious. This we have just observed.

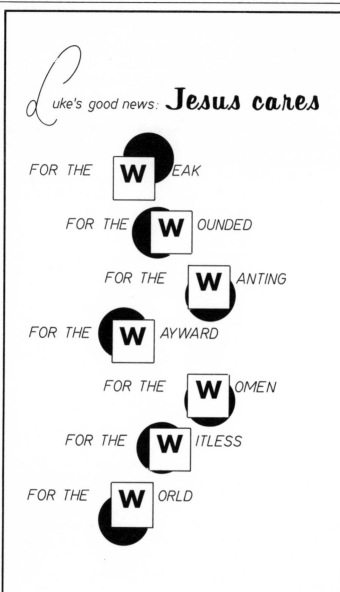

Luke's good news: *Jesus cares*

FOR THE **W**EAK

FOR THE **W**OUNDED

FOR THE **W**ANTING

FOR THE **W**AYWARD

FOR THE **W**OMEN

FOR THE **W**ITLESS

FOR THE **W**ORLD

Chart Number 6

6 / luke's good news

The reason Luke became a doctor was that he cared for suffering people. However, when he heard for the first time the story of Jesus, the Great Physician, told by Paul or someone else, he must have been so moved that the rest of his life had to be spent in telling others that JESUS CARES and cures. What "Amazing Grace! How sweet the sound!" This heartfelt concern for men is what impressed Dr. Luke. I suppose, if Luke had been a hymn writer, he would have produced a hymn like that of Frank E. Graeff, which raises the disturbing doubt:

> Does Jesus care when I've said "good-by"
> To the dearest on earth to me,
> And my sad heart aches till it nearly breaks—
> Is it ought to Him? Does He see?

And then Luke in the chorus would echo back his GOOD NEWS, with its answer dispelling all question:

> O yes, He cares; I know He cares,
> His heart is touched with my grief;
> When the days are weary, the long nights dreary,
> I know my Savior cares.

JESUS CARES so much, that His call goes out into the highways and the byways to compel the lost to come in. He is pictured in this Gospel as coming up to lepers and, where all other men have avoided them, touching them (Luke 5:12, 13). Some religionists might join in throwing rocks at them to keep them at a distance. Other men might force them to cry out, "Unclean! Unclean!" to warn of their presence. Not Jesus! He came toward them and reached out to touch them. Why? Because JESUS CARES. That is the story as told by Dr. Luke in the largest of the canonical Gospels.

Jesus Cares for the Weak

Luke was impressed that Jesus included those who might have been excluded by most people. Luke the Gentile is overwhelmed because he, too, is an outsider. We notice on the pages of this Gospel account that Jesus had included the WEAK. (See Chart #6.) To this day, the followers of Christ in their mission-outreach build orphanages for the outcast in pagan lands. In some places unwanted babies have been left by the side of the road to die from exposure. Are you caused to ask why Christians care for the kind of people who the "survival of the fittest" doctrine says should be forgotten? They care because Jesus cares for the weak.

When Luke began his narrative he did not start, as did Mark, with a powerful miracle by a mighty man. He started with an infancy narrative. He told of Elizabeth and Mary talking about the babies soon to be born to them. Luke's compassion showed through as he spoke sympathetically of the Lord raising the son of the needy widow of Nain (Luke 7:11-17) and Jairus' only daughter (Luke 8:42).

Jesus Cares for the Wounded

As the Lord cares for the weak, so He cares for the WOUNDED—the sick, the leprous, the broken. In Luke's work are remembered those such as the woman who had been bent for eighteen years, the man with palsy, and the soldier, Malchus. It is the latter, you remember, whose ear Peter had lopped off in the unsuccessful effort to cleave the man's skull.

Jesus Cares for the Wanting

Luke not only told story after story of Christ's healing power, but he also went on to make constant reference to the people who were poor—the WANTING—"the underdog." It is Luke who related the information that when Joseph and Mary came into the temple to offer a sacrifice for the baby Jesus, they could not bring a lamb for they were too poor. The most they could afford was a pair of turtledoves (Luke 2:22-24). It is Luke who preserves, too, Jesus' parable about Dives and Lazarus, a rich man and a poor man (Luke 16:19-31). In this human-interest story we sense that he was sympathetic with the poor man, even as he was in the examples of the unjust steward (Luke 16:1-13) and the rich fool (Luke 12:13-21). Luke includes the Isaiah reading in the Nazareth synagogue which foretold a Messiah who would bring good tidings to the poor. He writes about the concern of Jesus that alms be given those in want and that they especially be invited to the marriage feast. Those formerly excluded were assured inclusion in the love of Jesus.

Jesus Cares for the Wayward

I am lifted, personally, by Luke's further emphasis: Jesus cares for the WAYWARD. Here is the "High C" in the song of redemption. It doesn't matter who you are. It does not matter what you have done. It even does not matter into what depth of sin you have fallen. Christ's love will meet you there, reach you there, and recover you there. Did not the angel say to the hillside shepherds that unto them that day was born a "Savior," Christ the Lord? Did not Luke's passion story recall a forgiven thief on the cross? And did not Christ's loving glance speak acceptance to Peter at his denial? In between the opening and closing sections of Luke's narrative we meet hated tax men, like Zacchaeus, brought to Jesus as a further example that He came "to seek and to save that which was lost."

Jesus Cares for the Women

Another stress by our Gospel writer, Luke, is that Jesus also cares for the WOMEN (womankind). How in contrast was Jesus' attitude to the morning prayer of many Jews of that day who daily thanked God they were born neither Gentile, slave, nor woman. Jesus inspired His followers to teach that there was neither Jew nor Greek, male nor female distinctions in God's eyes (Galatians 3:28). Luke also is believed to have traced the bloodline of Jesus through His mother rather than through Joseph.

From experience, I know it costs money to travel as a preacher. I have wondered how Christ could take twelve men and go everywhere preaching the word. Who paid the bill? Luke 8:2, 3 answers this inquiry saying that women did. This has often been true, has it not? In mission work, women's groups have dedicated themselves to give their little; and that little, pooled together, became a lot and the work was done. How grateful we are that Jesus included women. Look at

Luke's stories of healing. Often it was such as that of a Syro-Phoenician woman—a non-Jew, and a non-male, i.e. someone previously considered an outsider. How Luke shouts this marvel of female inclusion!

Jesus Cares for the Witless

Go on to the fact that the master died for the WITLESS—those destitute of wit. He ministered to the foolish as well as the wise. Luke was an educated man. He may have studied at the University of Tarsus or the medical school of Antioch, if tradition is to be trusted. In all of his education he was overwhelmed by the reasonableness of Christianity, as the double volume of Luke/Acts shows. So even more amazing to him was the awareness that the "love of God all loves excelling," included both the wise (the philosophers) and also the foolish.

Jesus Cares for the World

If the other terms have left any class of people out, the next word will be all-inclusive. The love of God includes the WORLD. The message of God's concern is to reach all the nations beginning from Jerusalem (Luke 24:47-49). And following the Gospel of Luke, you must read the continuing account in Acts. Acts tells you how the story went at Christ's command from Jerusalem, the center of Judaism, to Rome, the center of the world. Luke prepared the Gentile, Theophilus, for the worldwide expansion in Acts through his earlier narrative, the Gospel of Luke. That Gospel heralded the exhaltation of such as the Samaritan by Jesus' descriptive "good." It recalled Jesus' observation that Old Testament heroes like Elijah and Elisha often brought their healing blessing outside Israel where faith was found. Paul's "beloved physician" placed Jesus on the stage of world history and not just Palestinian geography. Notice his opening chapter's references to Caesar Augustus, governing Quirinius, *et al.* Christ is for everyone. He cares for the whole world and every human being in it.

RESTORATION MOVEMENT
of Century One
John's Good News: Jesus Satisfies Our Longings

HE RESTORES

● *HAPPINESS to our marriages*

● *HEALTH to our children*

● *STRENGTH to our aging*

● *FULNESS to our hungry*

● *CALM to our fearful*

● *VISION to our blind*

● *LIFE to our dead*

Chart Number 7

7 / john's good news

The Gospel of John, the most loved of all the New Testament books, begins from eternity. Its opening words are "In the beginning was the Word." Its introduction ends, "And the Word became flesh, and dwelt among us" (John 1:1, 14). Yet, here on earth the glory did not shine through at the first. In John's account we see how disciples would be convinced one by one that this Jesus was a prophet, or that He is the Christ. But it is not until the very end of the story, after the resurrection event, that they have come to know who He really is. There Thomas cries out words of conviction that every Christian has come to address to Jesus, "My Lord and my God" (John 20:28).

The key verses of John, we have stated earlier, are John 20:30, 31. The passage says that out of the many miracles of Christ only a few (seven to be exact) have been selected. Through hearing these, the reader can also believe that Jesus is the Christ, the Son of God, and believing, can have life in His name. Just before this promise is made, John has recorded in verse 29 a significant and well-placed beatitude that Jesus had given.

While Thomas would not believe until he had seen with his own eyes and touched the living Lord with his own hands, that privilege was not going to be a possibility much longer. In the post-apostolic age, if anyone was to become a believer, it would be because of the testimony of somebody else from the first century. It could not be because his own eyes had seen, his own ears had heard, or his own hands had been privileged to handle Jesus, the Word made flesh (1 John 1:1-4). Pay attention to John's ordering of his material. First, John tells how Thomas was brought to faith by the miraculous presence of Jesus in the flesh. Next, he confesses that the blessed will be they who, not having seen Jesus, can believe in Him. And that means all of us who read John's Gospel in this day. We can have the blessing. And we will have the blessing when we come to believe through apostolic testimony. Lastly, John affirms that he is writing that apostolic testimony so we, too, can find the total salvation each disciple found in His name.

Briefly consider the seven miracles that John chose to use. If all Christ's wondrous acts on earth had been written, the world would not be big enough to hold the books about them. The apostle of love selected seven, for that is the number representative of totality. (See Chart #7.)

The seven miracles John records clearly indicate the extent to which JESUS SATISFIES OUR LONGINGS. He does this in a variety of ways.

He Restores Happiness to Our Marriages

The first miracle Jesus performed took place at Cana of Galilee where Christ turned water into wine (John 2:1-11). Here the start of a marriage celebration that could have been a catastrophe became a *happy* occasion. John does not record that one event as if it is the only time this sort of thing is going to happen. When you read the Gospel of John, what you hear internally is the voice of the resurrected Christ—the eternal Christ—sounding the truth again into your ear, "Your marriage can take on sparkle." Water always turns to wine when Jesus becomes the added ingredient in a newly founded home. John is not wanting you to remember only what happened long, long ago, as if it will never be repeated in your time. He desires you to know what Christ is available to do for you, right now! The "restoration" that is important here is the same as Psalm 23's "He restores my soul." When two people—man and wife—have their souls restored, their marriage is filled with that which is far beyond water—it is wine!

He Restores Health to Our Children

The second recorded miracle is about a man who had a sick child (John 4:46-54). The tenderness of God and the power of God are manifest in Christ's healing this nobleman's son. But we who read the story centuries after are to know that *our children* can find wholeness, wholesomeness, *health*— mental health, moral health—by the power of this living Jesus whose help is available at this hour.

He Restores Strength to Our Aging

The third wonder recorded is about a man who was so lame he couldn't get into a pool of water. According to the prevalent superstition, angels came down from Heaven to stir the waters. Only the first one in was healed. The rest of them were out of luck. I am so glad that God acts contrary to that common superstition and does not limit His blessing to the few who chance to win a gamble. In John's story in chapter 5, Jesus came to the man. He had for a long time had something to complain about. He had grown older and older with more and more aches and pains. Before He healed the man, Jesus asked if he really wanted to be made whole. Our hearts hear the same question as we read, "Do you want to be made whole?" Jesus, in Spirit, still walks through our world asking if we want wholeness. He offers, "I will restore *strength* to you." And a person who for many years has had wobbly legs, spiritually, and a bent back, morally, stands erect in the presence of sin. The man who has been blind to all the truth of God has his eyes opened. The man who from youth has had a leprous soul finds perfect cleansing. And a man long dead in sin rises to walk filled with life.

He Restores Fulness to Our Hungry and Calm to Our Fearful

The next two miracles are in chapter 6. There is the incident of the feeding of the five thousand. This is the only one of Christ's miracles recorded by all four of the Gospels. It is placed in the book to tell us that today all our *hungers* can be gratified—that we will find perfect *fulness* and satisfaction when we turn to Jesus Christ, the bread of life.

Right after that occasion, the disciples were returning at night by boat to their homeland. Christ came to them during a storm, walking on the water. They were all filled with fear. You can appreciate the dilemma if you have known the feeling of despair. The very sound of Jesus' assuring voice brought a sense of security to the disciples. His comforting words still reverberate through Christian centuries. They assure us that He can and will *calm* all of our *fears,* too, if we but listen to His voice.

He Restores Vision to Our Blind
and Life to Our Dead

Two more miracles are picked out of the many. One has to do with a *blind* man in chapter 9, and one has to do with *dead* Lazarus in chapter 11. The point of the telling is that whether you are blind or whether you are lifeless, Christ is the answer for you. He is the one who restores *vision*. He is the one who gives *life*.

Toward the end of John's entire book of the seven signs and the seven "I am" sayings, you meet up with a man named Pontius Pilate. This Roman governor heard who this Jesus is. He asked Him, "Are You a king?" Pilate knew what is right but he was not powerful enough in moral courage to do right. So he washed his hands of the whole affair. That story is told near the end of the book to remind each reader that he is either going to decide with Pilate or with Thomas.

When each man reads a Gospel account and hears "the gospel in the Gospels," he has come to just such a point of decision. He must say with Pilate, "I believe it mentally but I am not going to get involved," and try to wash his hands of it. Or, he must join Thomas down on his knees before the living Lord, confessing the words, "My Lord, and my God." God's blessing is for those who believe. The promise is given. Trust in Jesus and life will be yours. That is "the gospel in the *Gospels.*" Do you vote with Pilate or with Thomas?

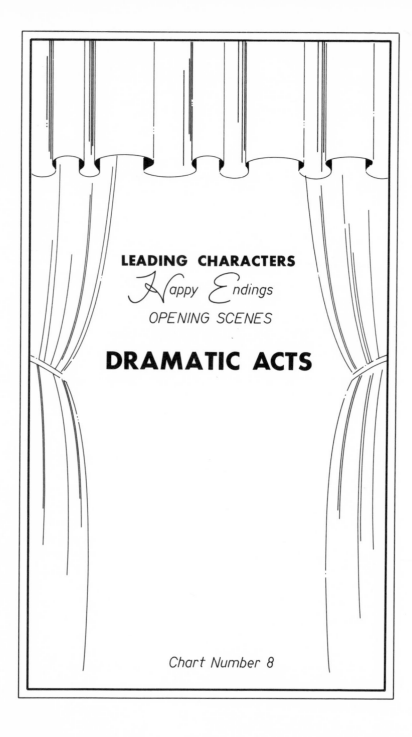

LEADING CHARACTERS

Happy Endings

OPENING SCENES

DRAMATIC ACTS

Chart Number 8

8 / acts

> Men's books with heaps of chaff are stored;
> God's book doth golden grain afford.
> So leave the chaff and spend your pains
> In gathering up the golden grains.
> Were all the world crysalite,
> The sun a golden ball,
> And diamonds all the stars of night,
> This book is worth them all.[1]

We are studying in this present volume the second half of God's Book that "doth golden grain afford," called the New Testament. We are treating it in its four parts: Gospels, Acts, Epistles, and Revelation. In the last part we searched for "the gospel in the *Gospels*." In parts to come we will look into the Pastorals (the epistles) for the pastoring to be emulated by our churches today and into Revelation, the last book of our Bible, for the revelation so needed in our present struggles of life. In this part we want to seek and find "the acts of the apostles" in this book called the *Acts of the Apostles.*

As you take your Bible now and turn to Luke's second volume, we intend to take the following four steps as suggested by Chart #8. First, we will take a good look at the main characters after whom the work has been named. We want to find out both who the apostles were and what their ministries were. We want to answer the question why, at this investigation, we should be studying neither the acts of elders and deacons, nor the acts of early disciples of Christ, nor even the acts of Christians gathered together for worship, but the acts of Apostles? Who were these men? What was their significance? We will find these men were not the only actors on the stage of early church history but they were the LEADING CHARACTERS in this dramatic book.

Some people have suggested that we should call this book the "acts of the Holy Spirit." That would be a suggestive and

---

[1] Author unknown.

significant title. Others have observed we ought to call this book "some of the acts of some of the apostles," or "a few of the acts of a very few of the apostles" in that only Peter and Paul really come in for much more than a mention. But I think it most appropriate that down through the centuries the church has called this book the *Acts of the Apostles.* As a body of men, the twelve and Paul (the apostles to the circumcision and the special apostle to the uncircumcision) are the significant persons in the guidance of the church after Christ had ascended to Heaven.

After we have discussed the leading characters, we want to talk about the six scenes into which Luke divided his material. This book spanned about thirty years of history and each geographic expansion, covering about five years of time, closed with a HAPPY ENDING. Luke has documented that, after the gospel had gone into a new section of territory for a particular period of time, there was success. He always concluded his selected material with what is called a "summary verse" or a "victory verse." These are the happy endings we wish you to note at the end of each of the significant geographical and chronological sections.

Thirdly, we plan to take a more exhaustive study of the OPENING SCENES—Act I and Act II, if we may so designate the first two chapters of Acts. Finally, we will look at the DRAMATIC ACTS of these apostles, inquiring as to their witnessing for Christ (Acts 1:8). What did they do with their eyes, their ears, their hands, their feet? We will learn more of their teachings in the epistles. Here we will search for more answers to the question, "What were the acts of these apostles?"

he Leading Characters
THE TWELVE AND PAUL

CHRIST CAST THE DRAMA
Especially selected _____

> 1 Corinthians 12:29; Ephesians 4:11;
> Luke 6:13; Galatians 1:1

CHRIST REHEARSED THE LEADS
Especially prepared _____

> Acts 1:3, 21,22; 10:40,41; 22:14,15; 26:16;
> 1 Corinthians 9:1; 2 Peter 1:16; Luke 1:2;
> 1 John 1:1

CHRIST ROBED THE ACTORS
Especially equipped _____

> Matthew 10:1,8; Mark 16:19,20;
> 2 Corinthians 12:12; Hebrews 2:3,4;
> Acts 2:43

CHRIST PROMPTED THE SPEAKERS
Especially needed _____

> John 14:26; 16:13; Ephesians 2:20;
> 1 Corinthians 2:9,10,13

Chart Number 9

9 / the leading characters

The LEADING CHARACTERS in the opening twelve chapters of the book of Acts are the twelve apostles, especially Peter. The second half of the book (chapters 13-28) follows Paul, the special apostle to the Gentiles.

In one sense, Jesus is an apostle. Hebrews 3:1 calls Him that, speaking of Him not only as our high priest but also as the "apostle" of our faith. Christ had been sent from Heaven on a mission to this planet. The Greek noun *apostolos* and the verb *apostellō* speak of "one sent" or "one commissioned." Since Jesus and other men besides Paul and the twelve were sent on missions, they may be termed in a particular way, apostles. In the New Testament Barnabas was called such, as was James, the brother of Jesus. However, Barnabas and James are not "apostles of Christ." They are apostles of the church, as Jesus was an apostle of God the Father.

Here, I want to limit our investigation of apostles to "apostles of Christ." After His resurrection, Jesus turned to His close followers and said, "As the Father hath sent me, even so send I you" (John 20:21). In the first case the Greek verb is *apostellō* from which comes our title "apostle." The second verb translated "send" is *pempo,* but it means the same. As the Father "apostled" Jesus, Jesus "apostled" the twelve and Paul. We speak in this chapter only about those apostles Jesus commissioned to do a very essential job within the kingdom of Heaven. Thus, the LEADING CHARACTERS in our present consideration in Acts are *the twelve* and *Paul.* Please turn to Chart #9.

Casting the Drama

The stage of the world is set. Here in human history the curtain is rising. The incarnate Christ one day will ascend into Heaven. Prior to this event He needs to pick men who will have a dramatic part to play in the extension of God's will on earth. Whom will Jesus select to be the players in the scene? It is not enough that the Jesus of the Gospels will give His life for our sins. It is not enough that He will conquer the grave. The people of the world will have to know about it before it can change their lives. Men will have to be *especially selected* to tell that story as witnesses. Thus, in the casting of the drama, Jesus selects twelve men. Look up the verses listed on the chart. Ponder each passage.

In 1 Corinthians 12:29 Paul raises the questions, "Are all apostles? Are all prophets? Do all speak with tongues?" And you know the answer that He expects is a negative answer: "Of course not!" God never intended that all should be apostles, or all should be prophets, or that all should talk in tongues. There are only certain men who are to be apostles.

The next text given is Ephesians 4:11, 12 where the same apostle has asked the Ephesian congregation if they did not know that when Christ ascended on high He gave gifts to men. He then continues:

> And he gave some to be apostles; and some, prophets; and some, evangelists; and some, pastors and teachers; for the perfecting of the saints, unto the work of ministering, unto the building up of the body of Christ.

The part of that passage that you want to put indelibly into your mind is the fact that only *some* were to be apostles. When Christ was casting His drama, He was selecting a very few out of the very many disciples to be these special emissaries.

The third passage for your consideration is Luke 6:13 that says the same thing as Matthew 10:1. There it clearly states that out of all of Christ's *disciples,* He picked twelve whom He designated *apostles.* If we would say jokingly that an epistle is the wife of an apostle, that would be inaccurate. It is equally inaccurate to think that disciples are the same as apostles. Out of hundreds of disciples only twelve were called apostles in the Gospels.

Galatians 1:1 was written at the end of Paul's first missionary journey, the expedition from Antioch of Syria to the cities of Galatia. The letter was an answer to the problems brought about by the Judaizers who followed Paul and upset his converts. These Judaizers asserted that Paul, not being one of the twelve, was not a true apostle. It is to defend the fact that he is indeed an apostle, a special apostle to the Gentiles, that he starts out the letter saying, "Paul, an apostle of the Lord Jesus Christ, not of man nor by the will of man but of Jesus Christ." Paul was claiming that he, too, like the twelve, had been *especially selected* to this ministry.

Other Scriptures should be studied here. Acts 1:2 talks about the apostles whom Christ "had chosen." When you come to the end of that chapter, you read of Matthias. You may have thought he has been selected by the one hundred and twenty in the upper room. Not so! Out of the one hundred and twenty only two were found that could possibly be apostles. Why? Only these two qualified as eyewitnesses of the risen Lord (see Acts 1:20-23). Then the persons in the upper room held these two men before Jesus in prayer. Their words were, "Lord, show us of these two, the one that You have chosen." Along with other requirements for anyone to be an apostle of Christ, he must be selected personally by Jesus.

Rehearsing the Leads

Now move to the second point of the chart. Christ not only CAST this drama, Christ REHEARSED these leading characters. Those who were going to be the official witnesses of Jesus were to be especially prepared so that they could do their particular ministry. Reread some background. Acts 1:3 tells that Christ appeared over the space of forty days to the ones He had chosen and He gave to them "many infallible proofs." Go now to verses 21 and 22 where Peter says that out of the group that had been with Jesus from the baptism of John one must be found to join the others as "a witness of His resurrection." You and I are neither "Jehovah's witnesses" nor are we "witnesses of Christ" in the Biblical sense. You and I can witness to an answered prayer. We can witness to the fact that it is a blessing to tithe. We can witness to any other experience that we have had. But not one of us can be a witness in the sense that the apostles were witnesses. Their eyes saw. Their ears heard. Their hands handled the incarnate Jesus after His resurrection (1 John 1:1-4).

Consider this: If Christ had risen but no men were eyewitnesses to that fact, how could we in the twentieth century be made believers? Christ appeared "not to all the people," reads Acts 10:40, 41, "but unto witnesses that were chosen before of God" and to these He made special appearances to equip them for their ministry.

It is true that Jesus appeared after His resurrection to women, early in the morning. It is true that on the same day in the afternoon He manifest himself to two on the way to Emmaeus. It is true also that He did appear to five hundred brethren at once. But He especially appeared to the apostles to make them the official witnesses to the central gospel fact that Christ conquered the grave. When Peter addressed the household of Cornelius and made it clear that Jesus did not appear to everyone but to the certain witnesses chosen aforetime, he adds that on these occasions Jesus ate and drank with them after He was raised from the dead (Acts 10:41). It is very significant that, when Christ made an appearance to the apostles, it was an eating experience. That carefully recorded fact guarantees that no one in our century, including Rudolph Bultmann, can sustain successfully that Jesus lived on only in their memory or as a spirit. The Jesus of the post-resurrection appearances was the same one, though glorified, who had dined with them around the table. Thus they once again ate and drank with Him, knowing well that ghosts neither get hungry nor have flesh and bones as they saw Him have. The living Christ, who dined with them in the upper room, also dined with them again at the sea of Galilee.

We are ready now for Acts 22:14, 15. Jesus has appeared to Paul and speaks: "The God of our fathers hath appointed thee to know his will, and to see the Righteous One, and to hear a voice from his mouth. For thou shalt be a witness for him unto all men of what thou hast seen and heard."

In Acts 26, Paul is giving testimony to his Damascus Road experience. You and I have never had an experience like that, because Christ is not converting the world by making special appearances. But, if He was going to make an apostle out of Paul, He must appear to him. No one can be an apostle unless he has had this experience of seeing with his own eyes the resurrected Jesus. So in Acts 26:16, Jesus' words to Paul are, "To this end have I appeared unto thee, to appoint thee a minister and a witness both of the things wherein thou hast seen me . . ." I'm trying to establish by these few Scriptures that in order to be an apostle, Christ's men had to be rehearsed by Him—trained by Him—to do the job of witnessing. Why? Because that is the job of an apostle.

First Corinthians 9:1 is an instance again of Paul answering the challenge of those who said he was not one of the original twelve and therefore not a true apostle! Paul raised some questions: "Am I not free? am I not an apostle? have I not seen Jesus our Lord?" The emphasis is upon eyewitness. Paul had seen; therefore he was qualified to be an apostle.

Second Peter 1:16 on our chart is Peter's claim to be an eyewitness of His majesty. Luke 1:2 shows that the author of Luke and Acts was not an apostle, though a very accurate historian. Luke claimed that many had taken in hand to write up this story and they got their information from those who were ministers and "eyewitnesses of the word." Luke had not seen with his own eyes but he had heard the testimony of those who had. As a careful investigator he affirms the dependable source of his information.

Finally, note 1 John 1:1-4. This is a passage from the great and last of the apostles who claimed his eyes had seen, his ears heard, and his hands had handled the living Word. He claims that he had ocular, auricular, and tangible evidence that Jesus Christ was alive.

Robing the Actors

We have said that these leading characters, about whom the book of Acts was written, were men especially selected and CAST for the drama. We have claimed further that they were especially prepared and REHEARSED for their leading part. We now add that they were then ROBED—robed as actors, robed with miracle power. If they were to be the official witnesses of Christ's resurrection, and their incredible gospel story to be made credible, they would need God to join with their witness. None of us wants to be a gullible believer. We need to have some substantiating evidence from Heaven. Thus when the gospel message was first brought as a faith "once for all delivered unto the saints" (Jude 3), God cooperated with the apostle's witness by giving a witness through miracle as these men delivered the new message. Thus Christ robed the actors, *especially equipping* them with miracle power.

Look now at Matthew 10, remembering that this was the ordination sermon of the twelve apostles. Matthew 10:1 tells how Christ picked out of all His disciples only twelve whom He called apostles. Verses 2, 3, and 4 give their names so there will be no mistake. Then the following verses go on to describe the apostolic assignment. We must listen carefully here to every word, lest today we try to do the unique ministry of the apostles—witnessing by miracles—which, if we try to do, we may fail to do successfully. It is obvious that I cannot do the distinctive ministry of Christ and die for the sins of the world. It ought to be equally evident that my ministry is also different from that of His unique apostles. We are *disciples* of Jesus Christ, not *apostles* of Jesus Christ. We are not assigned to bring a new revelation from Heaven to people. We are to talk the now "old, old story" of the cross and resurrection. We are just to retell it again and again. We are attempting to see with clarity how Christ robed these apostles. They were to be the special actors. They were the ones in the drama of history to tell the story of what Jesus said and did in their day. Verse 8 says that they will "heal the sick, raise the dead, cleanse the lepers." Since freely they had received, they were freely to give.

Mark 16:19, 20 are verses written after the death of Peter at Rome in A.D. 64. They record an accomplished event. Verse 20 reads, "And they went forth, and preached everywhere, the Lord working with them, and confirming the word by the signs that followed." If you read the context of this oft-considered "difficult passage," especially verses 9 through 20, you will notice that when the twelve apostles heard the testimony of Mary—that she had seen the risen Lord—they did not believe her (verse 11). The next paragraph tells about a further experience on the road to Emmaeus. When that report of Christ's resurrection was given by Cleopas and the other disciple to the eleven apostles, "neither believed they them" (verse 13). The paragraph that follows tells how Christ rebuked the apostles for their refusal to believe the witness of others, when the world would be dependent on believing their witness to the resurrection (verse 14). Next follows the favorite verses of so many people today—verses 17 and 18—speaking about picking up serpents and talking with other tongues and casting out demons. Jesus is giving a special promise to these qualified men as they go out to proclaim this message in their special role as witnesses. Finally, you arrive at verses 19 and 20. As you read, remember you are reading an historian's report about something that already had been accomplished. The Lord did work with these men and did confirm their word by the miracles that followed, just as He promised. If Mark was written near A.D. 64 as we have concluded, and if the book of Acts covers history from A.D. 30 to A.D. 63 (the end of Paul's Roman imprisonment), then every word in Acts is commentary on the meaning of Jesus' promise in Mark 16. What Jesus said would be the case, Mark is recording was the case.

Second Corinthians 12:12 finds Paul calling to the Corinthian mind their early Christian days when the "signs of an apostle" were wrought among them. In Corinth there were some who were questioning his apostleship since he was not one of the twelve. As a part of his defense he proves his apostleship with a variety of arguments. He was chosen on the Damascus Road. He was prepared by an appearance. And like the twelve, he was robed with the power, for he too could do miracles. These wonders were termed carefully by the inspired writer as "signs of an apostle"—not the signs of a divine healer, not the signs of a great believer, but the "signs of an apostle."

At this point, examine Hebrews 2:3, 4: "How shall we escape, if we neglect so great a salvation? which having at the first been spoken through the Lord, was confirmed unto us by them that heard." "Them that heard" would be the apostles, for it is they who heard and saw. Then it adds, "God also bearing witness with them, both by signs and wonders, and by manifold powers, and by gifts of the Holy Spirit." This historically accurate passage affirms that Christ first spoke the gospel, then those who walked and talked with Him (the apostles) passed it on to us. As they did, God was not silent. He joined His witness to their witness. He gave the signs and the wonders, and the works of the Holy Spirit.

Acts 2:43 is just one of the many passages of the New Testament that shows that the miracles were done either through apostolic hands or through those upon whom the apostles had laid their hands to give charismatic gifts. This passage makes the important distinction that the "many wonders and signs were done through the apostles" and not at this time by the hands of any of the one hundred and twenty who had been in the upper room, nor the hands of the three thousand converts who, hearing the gospel and repenting of their sin, had been baptized and had received the gift of the Holy Spirit. The miracles were done through the apostles.

If, in your mind, you are saying, "But Stephen worked a miracle and Philip worked a miracle," we agree. But we add, "They were selected as deacons and the apostles had laid on their hands and given to them a charismatic gift" (Acts 6:6). Even young Timothy, you remember, was told: "Stir up the gift of God, which is in thee through the laying on of my hands" (2 Timothy 1:6). The special men to bear the witness of Christ were the apostles and they were *especially equipped* with the power to do that task.

Prompting the Speakers

The final portion of the chart we are explaining speaks of Christ PROMPTING the speakers. If these are distinctive men (each one handpicked by Jesus), and they have distinctive marks (they have witnessed Him alive after the crucifixion), where is their distinctive ministry? They are to speak a message from Heaven. They are to reveal to the world the gospel. How will they speak? Christ will equip them. Christ will give them the message that is especially needed by the church of all generations.

John 14:26 was spoken to the apostles in the upper room just before Jesus went to the cross. The passage says the Holy Spirit will come in Jesus' place and will bring to their remembrance what He has said in their midst. No wonder John can write accurately his Gospel account maybe as late as A.D. 80-100—fifty to seventy years after the conversation took place. No wonder John can remember it so well that he can record the full conversations of John 13, 14, 15, and 16, plus the prayer of John 17, and not miss a vital word. The Holy Spirit, as promised, brought it to his remembrance.

John 16:13 was also spoken to the apostles in the upper room where Jesus said the Holy Spirit "shall guide you into all the truth." Now A-L-L spells a lot of truth. Christ's Great Commission ordered, "teaching them to observe all things whatsoever I commanded you" (Matthew 28:20). The apostles claimed, in the words of Paul, to have declared "the whole counsel of God" (Acts 20:27). If they were promised they would get *all* the truth and they claimed to tell *all* the truth as commanded, there is no other truth to be revealed in the centuries after the apostles put down their pens. There cannot possibly be a latter-day revelation, if the early revelation was true. It spoke of the apostles getting it *all*. Jude 3 agrees: "the faith . . . was once for all [time] delivered unto the saints." Through all the centuries that have followed since the first century, Christians have had the much humbler task of taking the ancient story and retelling it to the salvation of all who would believe. Nothing new need be added to replace, correct, or interpret it, for that once-for-all delivered message was eternal, accurate, and clear. Christians have, for nearly two thousand years, enjoyed the ancient gospel and with it we are satisfied completely.

Ephesians 2:20 tells us that our church is "built upon the foundation of the apostles and prophets." That implies that, as a Bible church, we are content with what the prophets of old had predicted before the Christ event, and what the apostles had preached as witnesses after that event. This apostolic and prophetic witness constitutes what we believe, i.e. the Bible revelation regarding Jesus. 1 Corinthians 2:9-13 reads:

> But as it is written, Things which eye saw not, and ear heard not, and which entered not into the heart of man, whatsoever things God prepared for them that love him. But unto us God revealed them through the Spirit: for the Spirit searcheth all things, yea, the deep things of God. For who among men knoweth the things of a man, save the spirit of the man, which is in him? even so the things of God none knoweth, save the Spirit of God. But we received, not the spirit of the world, but the spirit which is from God; that we might know the things that were freely given to us of God. Which things also we speak, not in words which man's wisdom teacheth, but which the Spirit teacheth; combining spiritual things with spiritual words.

In other words, God through the apostles gave to us the very "spiritual things" of the message, even guiding the "spiritual words" to express it, so that His church could depend entirely upon that revelation.

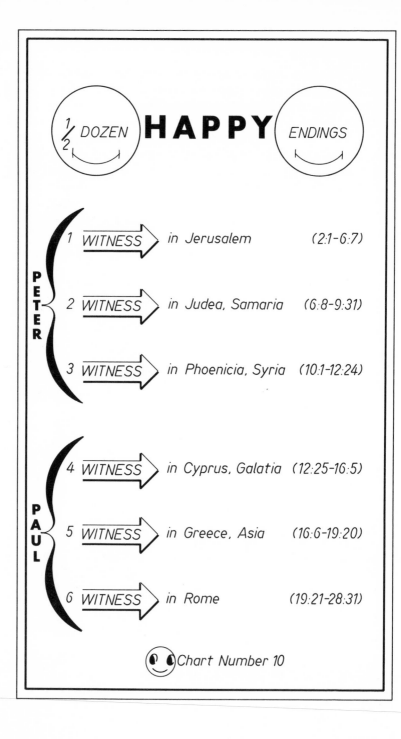

1/2 DOZEN **HAPPY** *ENDINGS*

PETER

1 *WITNESS* in Jerusalem (2:1-6:7)

2 *WITNESS* in Judea, Samaria (6:8-9:31)

3 *WITNESS* in Phoenicia, Syria (10:1-12:24)

PAUL

4 *WITNESS* in Cyprus, Galatia (12:25-16:5)

5 *WITNESS* in Greece, Asia (16:6-19:20)

6 *WITNESS* in Rome (19:21-28:31)

Chart Number 10

10 / the happy endings

We have talked at length about the "leading characters" in the Acts of the Apostles. This has been justified by the importance of these men. Without their testimony there would be no believers today, nor could there be. We need to progress now to Luke's outline by which we will trace their acts of witnessing.

In Chart #10 we present an outline of the book. We have here not an outline to be imposed upon the book of Acts, but rather an outline to be discovered by a careful analysis of Luke's material. The scroll on which Luke was going to write is estimated at thirty-five feet. He has many thrilling stories to tell, but available space limits our author. There are thirty years of church history from which to draw for his report. What shall he select to use? What shall he omit to tell? He appears to have decided to divide up his scroll into about six equal parts—approximately five years to each part. When he covers the first part, he will make clear the termination of that division or scene by a HAPPY ENDING. Then he will go to the next part and conclude again with another happy ending. He will do this throughout, as he shows the growth of the gospel both geographically and chronologically. He will cover six map areas and six calendar periods.

In the first half of the book, chapters 1 through 12, Peter is the main character. In the last half of the book, chapters 13 through 28, Paul will be the main figure. One point Luke desires to make evident to his readers is that Peter's gospel and Paul's gospel are the same gospel. They are of one heart and soul. They serve the same Lord. They do not create two churches, one a Jewish church and the other a Gentile church. They belong to the one body—the church of the living Christ.

Witnessing in Jerusalem . . .

Acts 1:8 is the key verse of this outline. It reads: "And ye shall be my witnesses both in Jerusalem, and in all Judaea and Samaria and unto the uttermost part of the earth." Section one, or scene one, will go from 2:1 to 6:7. You want to know, as you come to the period where the *witnessing* is limited to *Jerusalem* proper, "With what success was the gospel preached?" In the city where they were crying out a few days before, "Crucify Him!" now what is their cry? Look at our first summary verse, *Acts 6:7*. It is a victory verse—a HAPPY ENDING. "The word of God increased; and the number of the disciples multiplied in Jerusalem exceedingly; and a great company of the priests were obedient to the faith." So not only do you have the five thousand converts by Acts 4:4, you now have a number almost beyond comprehension. Then add to that the fact that even the priests—the Jewish religious leaders—had obeyed the faith.

What if you were told that a Protestant had become a Roman Catholic this very afternoon? Would the local newspapers even mention it? Probably not! But suppose the Pope of Rome or his Cardinals would come into the "Christian Church" tonight! Every paper in the world, including the Communist Press, would give the incident headline coverage. In Jerusalem, not only common men and women were coming into the church of Jesus, not only had one Jewish priest been converted to Christianity—a "host" of them had joined with the Christian cause. That is a summary verse. That is a victory verse. Notice that the *witness* goes first to Jerusalem, then northward to *"Judaea* and Galilee and *Samaria"* says the summary verse of *9:31.* The underlined passages in Chart #10 are the summary verses. The next section takes you farther northward yet, to *Phoenicia* on the coastline and to *Syria,* where the city of Antioch is located, from which community Paul is sent on his missions. You see that the first half of Acts is a northward movement from Jerusalem clear on up to Antioch of Syria, the first church where Jesus' followers were ever called by the name "Christian" according to Acts 11:26. Paul and Barnabas are in that congregation as the westward movement begins. Notice *12:24* in summary.

To the Uttermost Part of the Earth

The second half of our document starts at 4 on our chart. Here is the witness in *Cyprus* and the Roman province of

Galatia, Cyprus being just below or south of Galatia. Paul's long-range plan appears to be to take one geographical section after another, moving constantly westward, until the entire world knows of Christ. After the mission to Galatia is complete you have another summary verse in *16:5.* Paul had thought that upon taking his Lord's banner to Galatia, the next thing he would want accomplished was the reaching of the province of Asia. However, when he tried that, the door was closed. He attempted to go to Bythinia and Mysia but the doors were shut again and that by the Holy Spirit. You are acquainted with Acts sufficiently to remember the divine answer to his human dilemma was the Macedonian call, "Come over and help us." Thus the second missionary journey began. And it was not as Paul had anticipated, first Asia, then Greece (Macedonia and Achaia), but the other way around. We have come to call the mission to Asia the third journey. That is the way we moderns have come to talk of it. But the way Luke is thinking, he places the *Greece-Asia* section together all in one unit, although it was to Macedonia and Achaia first and then back to Asia. After Luke's summary verse, *19:20,* ends this movement there is one more, *28:31,* to follow and Luke's purpose will be accomplished. The gospel has finally reached Italy itself and *Rome,* the world's capital.

Christianity was never intended to be a Jewish sect. It was destined to conquer the whole world. And Luke's story shows that. Some people say Acts ends very abruptly with Paul in Roman imprisonment. But a second look manifests that the ending is not abrupt. Luke's planned goal was to show how the gospel got from the center of Judaism—Jerusalem, to the center of the world empire—Rome. Once that purpose was accomplished, Luke optimistically concluded his narrative with Paul in "his own hired dwelling" receiving visitors and in no way being hindered in his bold proclamation of Jesus.

From other sources you learn that, after his witness in Rome, Paul had further plans. These plans to go to Spain are expressed in Romans 15:28. As the ending of Acts anticipates and tradition supports, Paul is set free. He then makes this thrust into the extremities of the West. According to some in the Anglican church, Paul is thought to have gone beyond even this point as far as Great Britain. This may be doubted, but that Paul was planning a westward movement, with no intention of every stopping until death would stop him, sounds like the apostle reflected in the New Testament. "Unto all the nations" was the Lord's command ending Luke's life of Christ (Luke 24:47). The life of the early church marching out with that gospel northward, then westward, is the record of Acts. In Acts Luke has started a history of the Lord's church. But that history will never end until either Jesus rescinds His orders or the Church's mission is over because of the end of time.

ACT ONE

ACT TWO

$\mathcal{P}$reparation $\qquad$ $\mathcal{P}$roclamation

GET READY $\qquad$ GIVEN LANGUAGE

(1-11) $\qquad$ (1-13)

GET ON KNEES $\qquad$ GIVEN LOGIC

(12-14) $\qquad$ (14-36)

GET SET $\qquad$ GIVEN LIVES

(15-26) $\qquad$ (37-47)

TO GO

1   by recalling FACTS
2   by rehearing CHARGE
3   by reviewing EVIDENCES
4-5 by remembering WARNING
6-7 by rethinking GOAL
8-11 by reflecting PROMISES

Chart Number 11

11 / the opening scenes

Having refreshed our minds about apostles and their witness across the first-century world, we are ready to give closer attention to the beginnings of that world conquest that has not stopped yet. As Chart #11 suggests, we turn to Acts, chapters 1 and 2. For our purposes we will call these ACT ONE and ACT TWO.

ACT ONE—Preparation

The day of Pentecost, with its birth of the church, does not come until the incidents of Acts 2:1 and following. That means that all of Acts 1 is *preparation* for the commencement of the kingdom of Heaven. According to Luke's evidence and that of corresponding history, the church began at 9:00 o'clock, Sunday morning, May 28, in the year A.D. 30. (According to Leviticus 23:15, 16, Pentecost always fell on the first day of the week. The word *pentecost* means *fifty* and refers to the count starting after the Sabbath of the Passover.) In Jewish tradition that day became a celebration of the giving of the law at Mt. Sinai. It was the "fourth of July" for the Jews, marking the beginning of their nation. To Luke, Jesus was the real Passover sacrifice. Then the Pentecost that followed fifty days later brought, rather than ten stone-hard commandments from Heaven, the glorious Holy Spirit's descent. Did that old law in stone lead to the death of three thousand violaters in Exodus 32:28? Perhaps the three thousand who touched Christ by their faith and found life in Acts 2:41 are their anti-type. A "New Israel" having been created, the old Israel has become *passé.*

Get Ready

Act One gets the disciples ready for this wondrous day of Christ's coronation act. He first gets them READY, then ON their KNEES, and then SET TO GO. Verses 1-11 tell how Christ increased their readiness. He had spent three and one half years with them already. Now He will spend forty more days with them to get them better trained as to the nature of the kingdom of God. Thus far, they have been unable to comprehend the kind of kingdom Christ is going to set up. Their neighbors have been expecting an earthly Messiah. For the first time, after Jesus' death and resurrection, they really may be ready to accept the additional information. The subject to be studied is the "kingdom of God." The diploma to be given is the "Holy Spirit." The period of training is "forty days."

In the chart you see the first eleven verses subdivided in the rectangle in the lower corner. Verse 1 shows Jesus getting them ready by *recalling the facts* about what He did and taught in the days of His earthly ministry, as told in the Gospel of Luke. Verse 2 reveals a *rehearing the charge.* It speaks of them being commanded through the Holy Spirit in a commission. Verse 3 emphasizes *reviewing the evidences* of Christ's resurrection—telling how He appeared during a forty-day period with "infallible proofs" (K.J.V.). Verses 4 and 5 give Christ's *warning* which they need to *remember.* He told them "not to depart from Jerusalem" until they had received the "promise of the Father." Then in verses 6 and 7, the apostles are called upon to *rethink their goal.* They said, "Lord, dost thou at this time restore the kingdom to Israel?" He responds, in so many words, that this is none of their business. (That is almost a translation!) "It is not for you to know times or seasons, which the Father hath set within his own authority." He adds that it is rather for them to know they are to be His witnesses. In other words, they are to rethink their goal. It is not theirs to be date-setters, it is theirs to be soul-winners. And then the last part of this section, which recalls how Jesus got His men ready in verses 8-11, is where the workmen are to *reflect on the promises*—promises like, He will "come again" to receive them unto himself. Such full assurance completes their getting READY.

Get On Knees

In verses 12-14, you have a prayer meeting in an upper room—perhaps in the house of Mary, the mother of John Mark. There disciples are gathered to pray. It is to be noted that they are not praying for the Holy Spirit. They do not need to do that. They have been promised that He is going to come upon them. Christ will keep His word on that. They are praying rather to be ready for this event. Christ will be baptizing these apostles with His Spirit "not many days hence" (Acts 1:5). I believe that they are simply opening their lives, so, when the Spirit comes, they will be prepared for the Spirit's full power and effect. They are ON their KNEES (figuratively, if not literally) so that on Pentecost they will be on their toes.

Get Set to Go

They GET SET TO GO in the last half of chapter 1, where Peter points out that Judas has fallen away and their number has dropped to eleven. There must be twelve men. Otherwise, the imagery of the new Israel will be lost. If there were twelve tribes in old Israel, there must be twelve apostles as the new Israel commences. The group in the upper room find two are qualified and they ask Christ to make His choice through their casting of lots. The lot falls upon Matthias as verse 26 comes to an end in chapter 1.

ACT TWO—Proclamation

Chapter 2, as it opens, declares, "And when the day of Pentecost was now come, they were all together in one place." The verse just before has said, "the lot fell upon Matthias; and he was numbered with the eleven apostles." When the very next line after the "apostles" of Acts 1:26 says Pentecost was now come and they were all together in one place, the *they* likely refers back to the last noun, the *apostles.*

What is going to happen now in a book long called the *Acts of the Apostles?* These apostles are going to be acted upon by Jesus so they can act under His power. A room is filled with the noise of a wind marking the coming of the Holy Spirit. They are all "filled" with that Holy Spirit. They "speak with other tongues, as the Spirit gave them utterance" (Acts 2:4).

Given Language

We are now in ACT TWO. The curtain is rising on *proclamation.* First, they are given a LANGUAGE (verses 1-13). Judaism was for the Jews. Christianity is for the world. There are tribes, and tongues, and nations, and peoples. All of them are to be reached. How can these men, who are Galileans, go bear a witness everywhere that will be understood? God never gives any man an assignment without giving him the ability to carry out that assignment. God starts out by giving the commissioned apostles a language power from Heaven. Verse 4 says they "began to speak with other tongues, as the Spirit gave them utterance." Verse 3 reports that visible tongues appeared, "parting asunder, like as of fire" that sat upon their heads. Such a miraculous manifestation is appropriate to illustrate that theirs is a gospel to be communicated everywhere. And if, in their evangelizing, they ever need to talk in Coptic, in Latin, or in some other language or dialect, they will be given the ability to do their job.

So that Theophilus and all other readers will understand correctly what the gift of "tongues" is, as first mentioned in verse 4, Luke gives a clear explanation in verses 5-13. These men, without training, can now speak the wonderful works of God in all the languages of all the people gathered together from all these nations under Heaven that Luke names. Thus, from the first day of the church, recipients heard in their own languages what marvels God had wrought.

Given Logic

Not only were apostles given the LANGUAGE, as verses 1-13 reveal, they were given the LOGIC. They did not have to think ahead of time what they were going to say or how they would say it. It was given to them in that very hour (Luke 21:14, 15). This is evident when you look at Peter's sermon on Pentecost which has been preserved in brief in verses 14-36. What an introduction (verses 14-21)! What a proposition! "God hath made him both Lord and Christ, this Jesus whom ye crucified" (verse 36). What an array of supportive evidence (verses 22-35): First, the miraculous life of Christ (verse 22); second, the crucifixion and resurrection of Christ as witnessed by the Bible of olden times and the apostolic witness of New Covenant times (verses 23-32); and finally, the just-observed outpouring of the Holy Spirit by Christ from Heaven (verses 33-36). These are three proofs that Christ is indeed Lord (verse 36)!

Given Lives

From verses 37-47 we see that, as these apostles were given the LANGUAGE and the LOGIC, they then were given LIVES as their reward. Three thousand people came saying, "What must we do?" (verse 37) and they were told to repent and to be baptized (verse 38). And when they responded by repenting and being baptized, thus giving evidence of their faith, they received the gift of the Spirit as well as the taking away of their sins. And the Lord was said to have added daily to His body those that were being saved (verse 47).

DRAMATIC ACTS

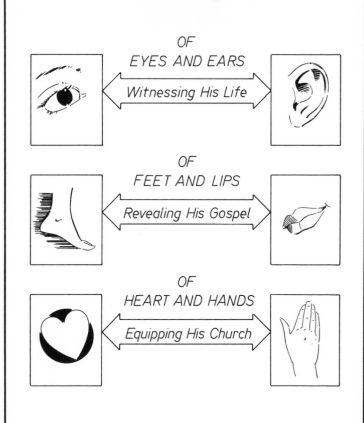

OF
EYES AND EARS

Witnessing His Life

OF
FEET AND LIPS

Revealing His Gospel

OF
HEART AND HANDS

Equipping His Church

Chart Number 12

12 / the dramatic acts

We have entitled PART TWO "the acts of the apostles in the *Acts of the Apostles.*" We have not sought for the common ground that all disciples shared in, although that is also found in this book. We have not searched for the duties or require- ments for elders, deacons, and teachers. We have looked for only the acts of these special men who were an essential link between all the believers of later days and Jesus Christ him- self. What were the ACTS of their EYES AND EARS? What were the ACTS of their FEET AND LIPS? What were the ACTS of their HEARTS AND HANDS? (See Chart #12.)

Witnessing His Life

We find that their eyes and their ears were to witness the life of Christ in a way that none of us from a later age can witness it. We are believers in the apostolic gospel that they passed on as witnesses of His majesty. It was the task of Peter, An- drew, Paul, and others to tell us what they saw and heard. That is the only source of information we have for the life of Christ. In curiosity, you may want to know a great deal more about Jesus than the apostles tell. But there is no other way to find out what Jesus did and said, except by these men who witnessed to what they experienced. First of all, the "acts of the apostles in the *Acts of the Apostles*" were acts of observa- tion, with EYES and EARS.

Revealing His Gospel

It is not enough, however, for them to have been witnesses *of* a fact. By necessity they must become witnesses *to* that fact, if men in other places and times are to believe. This is true because faith will only be created by hearing that word (Romans 10:17). Their FEET took them around the world. Their LIPS spoke out what they had experienced. My experi- ences may never prove helpful to you, nor your experiences to me, but the experiences of the apostles with Jesus offer help to us all. They went about and bore proclamation to the gospel.

Equipping His Church

What did they do because of their pastoral hearts? What did they do through the touch of their hands? As you answer these questions in the light of the New Testament book before us, stand amazed at the apostle Paul. Tireless he was. He "took on" no less than the whole world. He no sooner completed the first missionary outreach to Antioch of Pisidia, Iconium, Lystra, and Derbe than he returned immediately to confirm the churches in the cities from which he was driven out. Why? His HEART could not let him do otherwise. He went back home to Antioch of Syria and straightway wrote them the letter we call Galatians. He was using his HANDS to encourage, to write, to confirm, to strenghten, to ordain. When on later missions he went to Asia, or over the waters to Macedonia or Achaia, he would be found going back to ordain elders in all the churches. He would also use his hands to heal. He would use his hands to give one charismatic gift here, another gift there.

All the apostles—as men chosen of Christ, equipped by Christ, robed with power from Christ—left behind for posterity "apostolic Christianity." You and I are the heirs of that message. We have read today not a book entitled *Numbers,* but from the book named *Acts.* If your life was recorded in the Bible, where would friends think to look for your name? Would they search in a book of numbers in some local church that indeed believes in the apostle's testimony? Or would they immediately know you would be listed in a modern book of Acts, energetically promoting the spread of the apostolic faith?

> This is the Gospel of Labor—
> Ring it, ye bells of the kirk—
> The Lord of love came down from above
> To live with the men who work.
> This is the rose that he planted
> Here in the thorn-cursed soil—
> Heaven is blessed with perfect rest;
> But the blessing of earth is toil.
> —*Henry van Dyke*

Work!
Thank God for the swing of it,
For the clamoring, hammering ring of it,
Passion of labor daily hurled
On the mighty anvils of the world.
Oh, what is so fierce as the flame of it?
And what is so huge as the aim of it?
Thundering on through dearth and doubt,
Calling the plan of the Maker out.
Work, the Titan; Work, the friend,
Shaping the earth to a glorious end,
Draining the swamps and blasting the hills,
Doing whatever the Spirit wills—
Rending a continent apart,
To answer the dream of the Master heart.
Thank God for a world where none may shirk—
Thank God for the splendor of work!

—Angela Morgan
from "Work: A Song of Triumph"

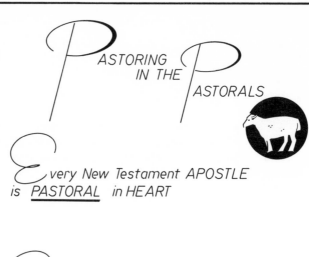

*P*ASTORING
IN THE
*P*ASTORALS

*E*very New Testament APOSTLE
is <u>*PASTORAL*</u> in HEART

*E*very New Testament EPISTLE
is <u>*PASTORAL*</u> in NATURE

*E*very New Testament CHURCH
is <u>*PASTORAL*</u> in NEED

Chart Number 13

13 / pastorals

No one reading this book today would claim to be the world's Messiah. Not one would purport to be an apostle of Jesus Christ and attempt to offer some new revelation to be confirmed by miracle. But I do hope that every reader, whatever his ministry, will seek to be in some sense a pastor. If you are not the pastor of a church or one who tends some Bible class, I still desire that you feel a shepherding responsibility toward the "small congregation" of your own family. Let us strive at this moment to be as practical as we can in our personal ministries as we study the "pastoring in the *Pastorals.*" (See Chart #13.)

It will be our aim to see in scope the epistles: i.e. the writings of Paul, of Peter, of James, of John, and of Jude. Find these personal or congregational letters in your own Bible just now. Turn to the concluding chapter of the book of Acts. Put your finger down at the beginning of the letter to the Romans. Next turn to the opening page of the book of Revelation. Glance back one page where you will find the final epistle of the New Testament, Jude. It is this rather small section of Biblical literature, from Romans through Jude, that we examine now to discover what PASTORING really is.

Since the middle of the eighteenth century, the term *pastorals* is a word that has been limited in usage to only three of the letters written by Paul: 1 and 2 Timothy and Titus. That is not the best possible name for these profound epistles, because Timothy and Titus, the recipients, were more than local pastors in the modern sense. They were apostolic delegates to the many congregations of Asia and Crete. To these Paul was ministering again after his Roman confinement had ended. While the two men were not themselves the pastors, as Paul's co-workers they were to see that pastoring was rightly done in every local congregation under their charge.

It is my belief, and the view presented herein, that every one of the epistles can rightly be called "pastoral." Each letter was written out of a "pastoral heart." Every one was sent because a Christian shepherd had concern for the sheep of God in his care. For the sake of the Master Shepherd not one lamb was to be allowed to go astray. Not one sheep was to lack proper feeding. Now we are ready to look at all of the New Testament epistles to learn more about the "pastoring in the *Pastorals.*"

In Part Two, we limited our study to the "acts of the apostles in the *Acts of the Apostles.*" We also could have hunted for the "acts of pastors in the Acts of the Apostles." We then would have turned to such Bible references as Acts 14:23. There it is stated that Paul, after he had established churches on his first missionary journey, began the second effort by returning to these newly established Galatian congregations. It was his purpose to see to it that they had pastors (elders) in each church. Why? Because sheep are dependent entirely upon caring shepherds. Sheep are not furnished with claws or talons to defend themselves. They are not provided with swift feet to run from a troubling hyena or a stalking jackal. They are dependent totally upon the "pastors" of the flock.

Had we turned to Acts 20 and followed Paul to Miletus, we would have found him on the beach meeting the Ephesian elders. We would have heard him define their shepherding task (verse 28): "Take heed unto yourselves, and to all the flock, in which the Holy Spirit hath made you bishops [overseers], to feed the Church of the Lord." And then he added a further duty for elders in verse 29. It is the warning that can be paraphrased, "Watch out for wolves!" Paul's words define an elder's threefold task: to watch himself, to watch his sheep, and to watch out for enemies of those sheep.

To give support to the men with such heavy responsibility, Paul ended his appeal to these Ephesian elders by advising, "And now I commend you to God, and to the word of his grace, which is able to build you up" (verse 32). Then holding out his calloused hands for all to see, he cried, "These hands ministered unto my necessities, and to them that were with me." What he was teaching the "teachers" was, "You have three tasks: Heed yourself, heed your flock, heed the wolves. You have three available and adequate sources of power to do that task: God, the Word of His grace, and just plain hard work." Today's desperate need is for well-shepherded congregations. If we are going to shepherd our churches, we first of all will need to realize that every New Testament APOSTLE was *pastoral in heart,* that every New Testament EPISTLE was *pastoral in nature,* and that every New Testament CHURCH was *pastoral in need.*

EVERY NEW TESTAMENT APOSTLE
is *P*astoral in Heart

*C*HRIST'S "UNDER-SHEPHERDS" were men of :

P ROCLAMATION

A FFIRMATION

S TIMULATION

T OLERATION

O BLIGATION

R ADIATION

Chart Number 14

14 / pastoral in heart

With the visual aid of Chart #14, look somewhat sermon-ically now at the very concept of a shepherd, or pastor. A pastor is one who stands in a pasture. A pastoral painting is often a depiction of a shepherd with his flock. The Bible is filled with passages using this image. In Matthew 9, starting at verse 36, Jesus describes the people as behaving like distressed and scattered sheep for they have no shepherd. In John 10, the Son of God makes the needed distinction between a hireling who works only for the money and a shepherd who cares for the sheep. In the scene of Psalm 23 all is well, because the Lord is the shepherd.

We need to ask if every New Testament apostle, evangelist, elder, and Bible teacher was a "shepherd at heart." The answer is a strong affirmation, "He indeed was!" But such an acknowledgement is of little practical alue unless we can move from the ancient apostles to the modern workers in today's churches. If all twentieth-century Christians, starting with you, dear reader, would become persons with "pastoring hearts," the church would be well on its way to renewal. We wish to make evident that EVERY NEW TESTAMENT APOSTLE IS PASTORAL IN HEART.

Proclamation

The pastors with "heart," for one thing, would feed their sheep. This means they would be men of PROCLAMATION. Sheep must have pasture. Their hungers and thirsts for righteousness must be satisfied by Christ's gospel. They must be led away from the poisoned waters of false teachers to the good food of divine revelation. Therefore, in the local congregations where you and I work and worship, your duty and my duty is to see that the people there hear the proclamation of God's truth. David wrote, "The Lord is my shepherd, I shall not want." Since you are an "under shepherd" to the Master Shepherd, may every disciple in your care be able to say, "I am not going to want. My teacher ever feeds me when I sit at his feet to learn from God's Word."

Are you a person of proclamation? Are you always giving out the gospel—the good food—the good news? We know that the word *gospel* refers to certain facts to be believed, blessings to be enjoyed, commands to be obeyed, and warnings to be heeded. Since this gospel is essential to man's salvation, we must faithfully feed the flock with that word. Because it is "good" news, we must place it before the sheep cheerfully. Heaven's orders are to feed the flock of God.

Romans 10:17 observes that faith or belief, comes by hearing. That is the only way it comes. Do all the little lambs and all the aging ewes under your supervision have the faith you want them to have? They can only get such faith by hearing strong proclamation of the Word of God. "Through the foolishness of the preaching," God has chosen "to save them that believe" (1 Corinthians 1:21). So, proclaim the Word in season and out of season.

Paul traces the fruit of salvation to the root of preaching in Romans 10:13-15.

> Whosoever shall call upon the name of the Lord shall be saved. [But] How then shall they call on him in whom they have not believed? and how shall they believe in him whom they have not heard? and how shall they hear without a preacher? and how shall they preach, except they be sent?

Note the links in this chain of logic. Whoever calls on the name of the Lord will be saved, but no man is going to call until he believes. Further, he cannot believe until he has heard. But, still further, there will be no hearing until there is proclamation and there will be no proclamation until preachers are sent out.

To what questions does this Scripture lead? Inquiries like: Mother, everyday are you feeding the little flock in the home that is your Bible class? Bible teacher, are you so preparing your lessons that, when the flock gathers around you, they will not go away hungry? Fathers, when your sons ask for bread, do you give a stone? We of the church must be people of proclamation. Each of us must join the apostles in acquiring a *pastoral heart* starting here and starting now.

I know that in Ephesians 4:11 only "some" were to be apostles, some prophets, some evangelists, and some were to pastor and teach. And yet, even if you are an evangelist, be pastoral. We have so many people who are brought into the fold who soon are lost to the church. If I should ask you how many converts you had last year in the congregation where you worship, you could perhaps give me a number. But of the others that were there already, did any get lost? At the local church where it is my privilege to serve now in an interim ministry, every Sunday night at 6 o'clock we have an "assistant pastor's meeting." To this gathering everyone comes who wants to assist in "pastoring." Anyone is welcome who knows how to write with a pen. We sit down and write love letters to absentees, love letters to shut-ins, love letters to prospects, *etc.* A church must be concerned about all the flock that is in its fold. A shepherd has to give an account for his sheep. He needs to remember that a prime responsibility of the shepherd is to feed the flock of God.

Affirmation

Referring again to the acrostic on the word PASTOR, be aware that every New Testament apostle was pastoral in heart. That is, he was a man not only of PROCLAMATION, but of AFFIRMATION as well. I hope that in your town your chuch is known, primarily, not for what it is against, but because of what it is for. A few years ago there was a popular song sung with lilting tempo, that went:

> Accent the positive,
> Eliminate the negative,
> Latch on to the affirmative,
> And don't mess with Mister In-between.

Do not allow yourself to stand behind the sacred desk in your church, or the podium in your Bible classroom, and condemn this and condemn that. If we do, the populace will think the church has only the bad news to tell of what is wrong. As Christ's people, we are not to be known for saying, "Look what the world is coming to." We are to be famous for declaring the good news regarding God's Son: "Look who has come to the world!" Let us be people of affirmation. Let us not negate and negate and then negate some more. Rather, let us affirm and affirm and affirm again!

Martin Luther contrasted the law of Moses and the gospel of Christ in the words: "The law says, 'Do this,' but it is never done. The gospel says, 'Believe this,' it is already done." Spare your listeners. Give them more gospel than law. Avoid stressing unduly, "Over you are the everlasting demands." In a discouraging world they need to feel the undergirding of God's assurance, "Under you are the everlasting arms." People, today, need shepherds who "shepherd." They need still waters and green pastures. They long to receive an anointing of the head with healing oil. They long for affirmation, not negation. As a hearer, I do not care to hear what you and your congregation are against. I want to know if you and your church stand for the gospel of Jesus Christ.

Stimulation

In the first century, and in our modern times as well, there is the need to acquire the apostolic qualities of PROCLAMATION, AFFIRMATION, and STIMULATION. I do not appreciate lazy preachers or elders. Yet, I know it would be better for one man to inspire ten other men to work than to try himself to do the work of ten men. Remember the advice in Hebrews: "Let us consider one another to provoke unto love and good works" (10:24). To *provoke* means to stimulate, to excite, to stir up. We need to do this provoking so that the brethren will get out of the grandstand as observers and into the game as participants. *Stimulate* one another to love and good works.

I pray that you do not try to do all the work in the church. I rather want you to practice a division of labor. The church needs you to help every man and woman, boy and girl find his or her work in some body of believers. Each Christian is in the ministry. Each disciple of Jesus has his function. In the imagery of 1 Corinthians 12, we are not all to be a mouth or an eye or an ear or a hand or a foot. But, we all are to fit somewhere into the body of Christ. There our function is to blend our talents with those of others to the blessing of the entire body. We are to find our place in the ministry. Also, we are to stimulate others in their ministry. Do what you can even this week. Encourage the others in your little circle to serve the Lord God.

Toleration

Our chart on PASTOR continues: Be a person of PROCLA-MATION, AFFIRMATION, STIMULATION—and underscore this one—be a person of *TOLERATION.* When a man goes to a foreign mission field, he must be a man of strong will and conviction. If not, he would never go that far from home at so dear a cost. We need such brave leaders. But, we also need a further quality of working together in harmony with others. We must operate as a family or as a team. Occasionally you hear about a church where there is friction between this elder and that one. Or you hear of hard feelings between a preacher and a congregation. Or, again, discord is reported between this woman and another one in the church fellowship. We, in humility, must learn to tolerate the other person's way of thinking.

You have been aware of the Great Commission, but have you ever heard of the "great permission"? I believe in Christ's Great Commission there is a great *remission* of sins as its primary result. There is also a great *emission* of overflowing by-products. But, in addition, there has been a great *omission* in too many of our lives. That omission is that we overlook the great *permission* to let another man do a particular church task in another way than we prefer it done.

We need "pastoral hearts." We need every elder to have such a pastoral heart. We need every Sunday-school teacher to have the same heart and learn to work with others. In the terminology of Alexander Campbell, study to obtain an "understanding distance" with the other man. Comprehend why he thinks like he thinks. Allow him to do God's work in the way he deems best.

Obligation

What must we have in the churches of today? Members of PROCLAMATION, AFFIRMATION, STIMULATION, TOLERA-TION, and OBLIGATION. These qualities are at the top of the "most wanted" list in all parts of Christianity today. Romans 1 gives you the three "I am" statements of Paul: "I am not ashamed of the gospel" (verse 16), "I am ready" (verse 15), and "I am debtor" (verse 14). Put under the microscope of your mind Paul's words, "I am debtor to the Jew and to the

Greek." This is not an outer compulsion! This is an inner compulsion! The church needs to sense its similar obligation to every member of the flock until none is uncared for.

Radiation

The sixth and final letter in our acrostic, "R," stands for the word RADIATION.

Years ago, as a student at Northwest Christian College in Eugene, Oregon, I was so glad when the evangelist "Willie" White would be holding a preaching meeting near by. I would make plans to drive out and hear him speak. There was something about that man that always has inspired me. He would step into the pulpit and his person just radiated. His face would light up with the glow of Heaven as he would rise to feed the gathered brethren. This glow is what we Christians must regain if we are going to win our generation to Christ. Condemnation does not win. Disharmony in the flock will not cause others to want to come take part. The world is attracted where the love of God is radiated.

I suggest that every day we ought to practice an immersion upon ourselves. We ought to baptize ourselves at least three times face forward into the beautiful thoughts of 1 Corinthians 13. Or, as someone else put it, "Every train of thought should be made to pass through the Grand Central Station" of that wonderful chapter on love. Love, as Paul defines it, is what too many lack. And yet, beyond all else, love is what attracts people to Jesus. When you radiate the love of God, people will come into the sheltering warmth of such compassion. Be PASTORAL IN HEART! Every New Testament apostle was! Every effective Christian will be!

Every New Testament Epistle
IS PASTORAL IN NATURE

MISSIONARY MOVEMENTS	PAUL	OTHERS
1st	*GALATIA* Galatians (49)	*James (49)*
2nd	*GREECE* Thessalonians (50)	
3rd	*ASIA* Corinthians (55-56) Romans (56)	*2 Peter (60)*
4th	*ROME* Colossians (61) Philemon (61) Ephesians (61) Philippians (62)	
5th	*SPAIN* 1 Timothy (64) Titus (64)	*1 Peter (64)*
	2 Timothy (67) (Hebrews) (68)	*Jude (67)* *John (80-100)*

Chart Number 15

15 / pastoral in nature

Read any one of these love letters, called epistles, in your Bible. When you do, you will find it to be written by a man who has a pastoral heart and who radiates the love of which we have been speaking. It matters not whether you read from the pages written by Peter, or James, or the author of Hebrews. Every last letter of the group has the same tone of love. Each epistle was called forth by personal concern for people. Every New Testament author so desperately cared for God's family that he could not forget the members of it. Consider Paul. Recall his ambitious goal of taking the gospel to the world. Remember his immediate objective of going to Rome (then to Spain, and then maybe to Britain). Then observe that he still took time to go back to some previously worked communities. He spent precious time to care for them, to confirm them or to write some encouraging letter to them. In the light of Paul's tireless example, dare not to say, "But we are too busy."

With the help of Chart #15, we now are ready to take a look at every New Covenant epistle as PASTORAL IN NATURE. In the chart it was necessary to arrange the epistles according to some system. They could have been ordered geographically, chronologically, alphabetically, topically, or in some other way. I have decided to list them by date of writing, full knowing that in every one of these instances the date might be open to debate. I choose not to give at length the different reasons for all of the dates to be used. Nevertheless, for the moment, we still will use the dating to which I cautiously and gradually have come. Be aware that we classify in one column the letters written by Paul and then in the other column the letters written by men other than Paul.

We begin by taking Paul's missionary plan as it moves westward from Antioch in Syria.

First Missionary Movement

The first missionary movement was to the area we know as Galatia. Do you have a map in your Bible? You might want to look at the Roman provinces. From the city of Antioch, in the Roman province of Syria, Paul is going to move westward to the area termed Galatia and the island just south of that called Cyprus. Then he will intend to go to Asia, the next Roman province, but the call of the Macedonian will take him across the Aegean Sea first to Greece. This we will call the second missionary movement or journey. The third outreach is Paul's return back to cover the Roman province temporarily omitted by divine intervention—that of Asia. And, though we usually do not call the following move a fourth missionary journey, Paul's trip to Rome is exactly that. The government may consider Paul a prisoner being shipped to Rome for trial. As far as he is concerned, he is going to Rome to bear witness to Jesus Christ. And since in the book called Romans Paul has declared his intention after Rome to go to Spain, we will call that effort the fifth of his missionary endeavors. It is my opinion that he accomplished that dream of evangelizing Spain before he came back to Rome. There, according to tradition, he was killed in A.D. 67. Thus in Chart #15 we have placed the apostle Paul's five thrusts westward from Syrian Antioch.

I want us now to place the letters Paul wrote into the time slot of each of these journeys just defined. By putting these epistles in historic setting, I want you to see something important. After Paul has brought these people of the Roman world into God's fold by making them Christians, he then goes back and shepherds them. He does this by his pen when he cannot do it by his presence.

It is my conviction that the first epistle that Paul wrote was *Galatians.* Paul's first Gentile mission was into Galatia. There he established churches in Antioch of Pisidia, Iconium, Lystra, and Derbe. He was driven out of each city, one by one, through Jewish opposition to the new faith. Nevertheless, immediately he goes back to each one of these cities. He returns to the churches with the purpose of strengthening and confirming them. When he gets home to the sending church in Syria, he hears some bad news. Paul has gone to Gentiles and preached the gospel. Many of them have believed it and have responded to it in baptism. They have become Christians. But since that time, other and later "evangelists" (called Judaizers) have come in from Judea.

They have told these same people, "It is not enough that you have believed in Christ and have been baptized. You also must be circumcised and keep the law of Moses to be saved."

When Paul hears that this has happened, he takes pen in hand and writes the little letter we call *Galatians.* Paul claims that these false teachers are "perverting the gospel" of Christ. He warns that if even an angel from Heaven comes and gives such a different gospel than that originally delivered them, that teacher should be anathema (Galatians 1:6-9).

It is Paul's argument in the book of Galatians that Christians are free from the law of Moses. Abraham was saved by faith "four hundred and thirty years" before the law of Moses ever existed (Galatians 3:17). Paul looks at the law as a tutor whose job was to prepare for the Master Teacher (Galatians 3:24). The application is that, since the "faith [Christianity] is come, we are no longer under a tutor [Judaism]" (Galatians 3:25). In this "pastoral" letter of Galatians, by various arguments and illustrations, Paul claims that we are free from the law and that we are saved exclusively by the gospel (Galatians 5:1-4). So we conclude that in the year A.D. 49, at the end of the first missionary journey, Paul writes from Antioch of Syria the Galatian letter.

In your Bible this would place the writing of Galatians just before the beginning of Acts 15. We say this for the reason that Acts 14 is the Galatian mission and Acts 15 is the Jerusalem conference. That assembly was called to face the problem raised by these Judaizers. Since Paul makes no reference to the conference in his letter, we are driven to the decision that it has not yet been held. From that conference in Acts 15 other letters go out to the troubled churches saying that James agrees, Peter agrees, the twelve apostles agree with what Paul has said and done. It is the gospel alone by which we are saved, not by the works of the law. The first mission, the mission to Cyprus and Galatia, produced one letter from Paul, the Galatian letter.

Second Missionary Movement

Let us proceed now, by the aid of Chart #15, to the second journey. The second mission took Paul to Greece, to the northern section known as Macedonia and to the southern section known as Achaia. After the Macedonian call that pulled Paul out of Asia, he went by way of Neapolis to the Macedonian city of Philippi. There he founded the church as recorded in Acts 16. From Philippi, Paul worked southward to establish churches in Thessalonica, Berea, Athens, and finally Corinth. All this he accomplished before he sailed to a festival in Jerusalem.

On his second journey, Paul wrote two letters that are still with us. Both of these were to the new Christians in Thessalonica. We call the letters *1 and 2 Thessalonians.* We will date both of these at around A.D. 50, one year later than Galatians. In these letters Paul is concerned about some Christians God has made through his preaching in Thessalonica. He has heard that they are disturbed regarding the second coming of Christ. Some of their brethren have died. Their loved ones are saying, "Are these who have died going to lose out on sharing with Christ at His second coming?" So 1 Thessalonians comes from Paul's hand as another instance of pastoral concern. He writes to say that "the dead in Christ shall rise first; then we that are alive, that are left, shall together with them be caught up in the clouds, to meet the Lord in the air: and so shall we ever be with the Lord" (1 Thessalonians 4:16, 17). Paul is asking them not to worry if they die before the return of the Lord. Every one of the five chapters of 1 Thessalonians ends with something about the return of Jesus, the *Parousia*—1:10; 2:19, 20; 3:13; 4:13-18; 5:23.

The only reason Paul wrote a second letter to the same people on the same subject was that some had misunderstood the first epistle. They had understood Paul's affirmation of Christ's return as an acknowledgement that Jesus would come back immediately. In the second Thessalonian letter Paul is asking them not to think of Christ's coming as "just at hand." Rather, they are to be aware that certain things have to happen first. This is especially the emphasis of the earlier verses of chapter 2.

Review what we have said thus far in our study of the epistles. We have asserted that Galatians and Thessalonians were written because a man cared about people made Christian. Paul had not just held an evangelistic meeting, left town and said, "Now, it is all up to the elders." Paul so cared for those people, he went back to visit them. He wrote letters to them to show evidence of his "pastoral heart."

Third Missionary Movement

Go to missionary journey three as listed on Chart #15. Note that it took Paul to Asia. The main city in Asia was Ephesus, as you know. Trace Paul's journey on your map. After he left his Grecian work from the city of Corinth, he traveled by boat from the port-community of Cenchrea, through a temporary stop at Ephesus, to a feast in Jerusalem. Then he went back again to Ephesus to work for three years out of this capital city of the Asian province. At his first stop there, he had left two people to start the work for him. These were the friends he had made in Corinth, Priscilla and Aquilla. The mission began in their home. It is said in Acts 19:10 that when Paul got to working in this province, in two years all Asia heard the gospel. What an evangelist he was! What inexhaustible strength he possessed! But, for our purpose now, note that on this particular mission three New Testament letters were written that we still have—1 and 2 Corinthians and Romans.

First Corinthians was written in A.D. 55. Paul had no sooner come from Corinth, via Jerusalem, to Ephesus than he heard about some trouble in the Corinthian church. He sincerely cared for these people, busy as he was in Ephesus. With all the work to be done there, he still took time to write back to the Achaian church.

What was the purpose of 1 Corinthians? It was to answer both their questions and their problems. Christ's people in Corinth had troubles, and "pastor-hearts" care about troubled sheep. The outline of the book you know already and you know it well. Paul simply talked about first one problem and then another. The first four chapters of 1 Corinthians contain Paul's answer to the problem of division. Chapter 5 responds to the problem of immorality within the congregation. Chapter 6 is Paul's reaction to the problem of lawsuits in secular courts between believers. Chapter 7 deals with the problem of marriage during a time of crisis. Chapter 8 faces the problem of eating meat that has been offered in worship to idols. Chapter 9 handles the problem of paying the preacher (pause while that soaks in). Chapters 10 and 11 treat the problem of proper decorum in public worship. Chapters 12, 13, and 14 are about the problem of the proper use of charismatic gifts. And chapters 15 and 16 are the apostle's answer to the problem of maintaining faith in the resurrection. Paul wrote this first Corinthian letter from Ephesus where his next mission after Greece had taken him.

Second Corinthians was written approximately a year later, A.D. 56. This was while Paul was on a confirmation journey that temporarily took him back through Macedonia. Once again in his life he was forced by the undermining tactics of Judaizers to write and justify his apostleship. On this same confirmation tour, after Paul had dropped down from Macedonia to Corinth, he there produced the Roman letter. He was at that time anticipating his future ministry to that great city in Italy. He wanted on record in the capital city of the Roman Empire, a document that declared his gospel that, while all men were lost in sin (Romans 1-3), all men could be saved in Christ (Romans 4-8). The letter vindicates God's rejection of the Jews (Romans 9-11) and manifests the moral character of life under faith rather than law (Romans 12-16).

Fourth Missionary Movement

On every journey Paul checked on the people he had won to Jesus. When he could not get to them in person he had plenty of writing materials and he wrote letters. Fortunately for us these few letters by Paul have been preserved. He must have written many that now are lost to us (see 1 Corinthians 5:11). But for this fourth outreach mentioned on Chart #15, he went to Rome. There he created what we have come to call the "prison epistles." It is in Acts 28 that we read about this imprisonment of Paul. He had been captured in Jerusalem, then kept in jail for a while in Caesarea. There he made the appeal to Caesar which led to his transfer to Rome. We generally date this two-year confinement in Rome at A.D. 61-63.

Arbitrarily, we are dating three of these four prison epistles in A.D. 61. All we really know is that three letters were written about the same time and possibly on the same day. The three are *Colossians, Philemon,* and *Ephesians. Philippians* was written at a later time. We note this for Philippians is filled with an optimism of expected release from that Roman imprisonment. So to make it easy to remember, we will use dates like A.D. 61 for Colossians, Philemon, and Ephesians, and A.D. 62 for Philippians.

What is the story behind the writing of Colossians, Philemon, and Ephesians? Paul is in prison. A pastor from the Lycus Valley in Asia does not know what to do. A heresy has started to arise. The preacher does not see how to handle it himself. But he knows Paul will know how to deal with it. The preacher's name is Epaphras. His church is the Colossian congregation. These saints at Colossae likely gathered in the home of Philemon, a slave master in the city. Epaphras reasons within himself, "I've got to get out of here, work my way to Rome, and ask Paul what to do with the rise of this new teaching before it destroys my church." Here again, note the pastoral concern. Epaphras gets to Rome. He does find Paul and the Colossian letter of four chapters is the result.

Since Tychicus, the *amanuensis,* or secretary, is going to be bearing the letter all the way to Colossae, Paul might just as well meet another need. At this same time he will return a runaway slave, whom he has converted, to his legitimate master. He will do this under Tychicus' supervision. The slave's name is Onesimus. His master's name is Philemon, the man in whose home the Colossian church has been meeting. Thus the letter to Philemon is written and sent on the same occasion as Colossians.

Paul, in the light of these circumstances, sees a further opportunity to pastor God's flock. As the slave, Onesimus, and the letter-bearer, Tychicus, travel to Colossae, they will be passing through Ephesus on their way from the sea into the Lycus Valley of Asia. Hence, we have a letter to the Ephesians borne by the same man. The similarities of thought and wording between Ephesians and Colossians are understandable in the light of the fact that both letters were written from the same place at the same time.

Underneath all these remarks I am making is this single fact: In Paul we find one Christian worker who cares so much for people he has won to Christ that he cannot forget them. He does not follow the practice of some: "Win 'em, dip 'em, and drap 'em." Rather, he wins them, baptizes them, writes to them, visits them, and, the rest of his life, prays for them.

Some time before Paul was released from this Roman imprisonment, he wrote the little Philippian letter. You may remember when that congregation started. Its founding is told in Acts 16 where the charter members are shown to be Lydia and her household and the Jailor and his household. The Philippian epistle is written to this church that, from its very beginning, contributed once and again to Paul's ministry. So, as you might expect, Philippians is a "thank-you letter." They had sent by Epaphroditus some supplies to Paul in his Roman imprisonment. Our letter to the Philippians is Paul saying, "Thanks a lot!" It is our fourth and last prison epistle.

Fifth Missionary Movement

We come now to those three letters by Paul that are commonly termed "Pastoral." They force us to make a determination about Paul's death. Does Paul get to Spain? This is tradition. It is not Biblical record. Personally, I think it is dependable tradition. If it is, and Paul is released from the prison of Acts 28, is he ready to go do what he has intended to do for so long? He had expressed his plan of going to Spain in the Roman letter (Romans 15:28). Some believe that somewhere around A.D. 63, in preparation for that adventure, Paul went to Crete to leave Titus (Titus 1:5). He traveled on to Asia to leave Timothy (1 Timothy 1:3). He then worked his way around to Dalmatia, where he spent the winter (Titus 3:12). Next, he headed toward Rome where he conversed with Peter and then went on to Spain. It may be that the reason Paul was not killed during the Neronian persecution of A.D. 64 was that Paul was off in distant Spain at the time. It was then that Peter was crucified upside down in the city of Rome according to tradition. If this chronology can be made reasonable, the dating of the letters to Timothy and Titus given here will stand.

What you have in *1 Timothy* and *Titus* are written credentials for two men. The authorization is to enable them to carry out a mission assigned them for the period of Paul's absence in the West. While Paul will be in Spain, Titus will supervise Crete and all the churches there. Timothy will watch the Asian field, working out of the base in Ephesus. Having put his workers where he wanted them in his absence, Paul moved into Macedonia. It was there Paul wrote to Titus and to

Timothy in the communities where he had left them. The purpose of 1 Timothy and Titus was not to tell them for the first time what to do. He had already given them their oral instructions. He desired to put his orders in writing now. Thus, if somebody in the church should say, "What do you young whippersnappers think you are doing, telling your elders how to act?" they would have a written document to show their authority. Our conclusion is that the letters of Titus and 1 Timothy, written by Paul in A.D. 64, are credentials to set the churches in order (Titus 1:5). This is the mission of the men named in the documents.

It is only when Paul comes back from Spain that he is captured and put in solitary confinement in Rome. It is from this final imprisonment that he writes his "swan song" of 2 Timothy. It is about the year A.D. 67. Not long after he puts his worn pen down, one of the greatest lives in human history is snatched away at the execution block. Only then does Paul's writing of pastoral letters come to an end.

On Chart #15 you will find one other letter in the column referring to Paul, but it is in brackets. It is the book of Hebrews. In the light of Hebrews 2:3, 4, it appears that Paul, himself, did not write this letter. Some associate of his apparently did. In chapter thirteen you find Paul's friend, Timothy, mentioned as a co-worker of the author. Whoever wrote Hebrews (Apollos?) also wrote out of a "pastoral heart."

What is the theme of this sermonic letter? It is written to Jewish congregations in Rome that have converted to Christ and are now Christian churches. Remember when Nero played his violin and blamed Rome's fire on the Christians? Under that Neronian persecution that broke out in A.D. 64, these formerly Jewish synagogues—but now Christian churches—are tempted to go back into Judaism. The Jews are not being persecuted; the Christians are. So the author of our letter writes in A.D. 68 to say, "If you go back into Judaism, you have left the best for something far less than that. You have reverted from the saving gospel to the law that cannot save." His strong arguments are: Christ is superior to the revealers of the Old Testament times (chapters 1 and 2), to the deliverers of the Old Testament days (chapters 3 and 4), to the priests of the Old Testament period (chapters 5, 6, and 7), and to the covenant of the Old Testament dispensation (chapters 8, 9, and 10). The last three chapters (11, 12, and 13) plead with the people not to give up their faith, their hope, or their love. It is an appeal to stay true to Jesus Christ whatever the cost. It is another letter of "pastoral" care.

Epistles by Other Authors

For more detail on individual books we must wait until some later occasion. If not, we may forget our present purpose of seeing all the New Testament epistles at once in scope. We must not fail to observe that each letter was written in "pastoral" concern. Refer again to Chart #15. Find at A.D. 64 in the right column the letter called *1 Peter.* Try to remember this: the letter we have come to title *First* Peter likely was written after the letter we term *Second* Peter. If you do not remember that, you could have problems with the apostle Peter's authorship of 2 Peter.

During our consideration of 1 Timothy and Titus, we have already referred to the fact that Paul went through Rome on the way to Spain after he had revisited such places as Crete, Asia, Macedonia, and Dalmatia. He apparently found Peter in Rome on this occasion. Now I am not saying Peter was Pope of Rome, nor that he ministered there for twenty-five years. Neither of these statements is true. I am saying that Peter did get to Rome during his lifetime. He was crucified there in A.D. 64, according to strong tradition. As Paul passes through Rome on his way to Spain, I think he requests Peter, in his absence, to watch out after his churches throughout Cappadocia, Pontus, Galatia, Asia, and Bythinia. This is a request similar to that assigned Titus regarding Crete and Timothy regarding Asia. So Peter does write to congregations established by Paul's workers in that area near the Black Sea. He writes to encourage fellow-Christians in a time of growing Neronian persecution. That is the point of the message of the letter we label 1 Peter.

Long before that incident, Peter wrote what we today call *2 Peter.* That epistle was penned as early as A.D. 60, while Peter was living and working in Jerusalem with the apostles. We only call this "Second" Peter because it is the shorter of the two letters. It was placed in your Bible after the other composition by Peter because of its size. Maybe you noticed that the last letter of the Pauline collection is Philemon. It, too, was placed last because it is the shortest. It was not placed last because it was written later than 2 Timothy. Neither is Romans placed first because it was the earliest of Paul's letters, as reference to the chart will show. The present arrangement of the books in the New Testament has nothing to do with time of writing. Second Peter is a prophetic warning to Christ's disciples of coming false teaching. It needs to be read in relationship to Jude for much of it is word for word. The difference is, 2 Peter is prophecy of what will come to pass. *Jude* is a tract calling believers' attention to the earlier letter by Peter, now fulfilled.

Peter's death comes in A.D. 64. Jesus' brother James is martyred in A.D. 66. Paul's decapitation occurs in A.D. 67. After the demise of these giant church leaders, Jude sends out his tract in A.D. 67. He points out that the warning prophecies of Peter (2 Peter) and the other martyrs were now being fulfilled. Jude urges the church to be alert, prepared, and faithful.

James probably wrote his epistle in A.D. 49 before the church ever had gone to the Gentiles. *James* was addressed to the Jewish Christians in a dispersion. This is likely the one mentioned in Acts 8:4. There, you remember, the apostles are reported to have remained in Jerusalem, while the other Christians were "scattered abroad" going everywhere "preaching the word." James who has pastored these people for many years, still cares about them even though they are far away from his sight. Enough time has passed that they are waning in their earliest zeal. James, therefore, starts out to give these dispersed Jews twelve moral maxims they should heed as the new "twelve tribes" of Israel (James 1:1).

The last epistles in our Bible, *1, 2,* and *3 John,* were near the end of the first century. These, like all the rest, are the love letters of a pastor who cares for his people. He endearingly terms them his "little children." John's epistles, like his Gospel, are protecting the ones under his care from fallacious concepts like those crystalizing into the Gnostic heresies of a later century. No shepherd who cares for his sheep leaves them uncared for when wolves are about.

$\mathcal{E}$very New Testament CHURCH
is _PASTORAL_ in NEED

$\mathcal{P}$astors are

ESSENTIAL

to a church's well-being

TITUS 1

Shepherds are essential
(5)

Qualified shepherds are essential
(6-9)

Functioning, qualified shepherds are essential
(10-16)

Chart Number 16

16 / pastoral in need

It is my prayer that you will reread all of the epistles and that their restudy will help expose three certain truths. I want you to remember that "every apostle was pastoral in heart." I want you never to forget that every epistle was addressed to a real-life situation in the early church, making the correspondence "pastoral in nature." I want you to realize that EVERY NEW TESTAMENT CHURCH, like every congregation on earth today, IS PASTORAL IN NEED. As we examine Chart #16, the last in Part Three, turn with me to that little book called *Titus.*

Shepherds Are Essential

For this brief study look only at Chapter 1 in this epistle. Even leave out of that chapter the lengthy salutation in the first four verses. I want to suggest that *pastors are essential to a church's well-being.* Pastors, in New Testament parlance, are the elders. A church can exist without elders. We know that because in Acts 14 Paul went into territory in Galatia to establish churches and only later did he come back to "appoint elders" (Acts 14:23). What is the necessary conclusion? The church existed in Galatian cities before an eldership was created in those places. But, while an eldership is not essential to a church's being, experience proves that it is essential to its *well*-being. You can have sheep without shepherds, but sheep *need* shepherds!

I could take you through 1 Timothy, chapter 3, where Paul writes at length on the office of bishop and deacon. I choose rather to turn to the much shorter Titus 1:5-10. Those few verses are sufficient to carry the point. Look at verse 5 where you read:

> For this cause left I thee in Crete, that thou shouldest set in order the things that were wanting, and appoint elders in every city, as I gave thee charge.

That is to say, Paul does not want any congregation to have

any needs unmet. They definitely need elders. Therefore, Titus is to see that elders are appointed in every town. As Titus fulfills his mission to Crete, he is to go across the entire island. He is to proceed city by city. The words "every town" in Greek are *kata polis*—every city. Titus is to go from one end of the island to the other. It is Paul's admonition that every cluster of Christians have an eldership. We notice that the elders are to be "appointed." That is the word *kathistēmi.* Some Bible commentators refer to Acts 14:23 where elders also were "appointed." There a different Greek word, *cheirotoneō,* is used and may reflect how the selection was made. The latter Greek word may mean that the people were to "reach forth their hands" in vote for the persons they wanted to be their shepherds. At least the text does not call for just one elder to be chosen in every congregation. It expects a plurality of elders to be found. The elders are visualized to be a body of believers so respected by the other sheep that they will be called out to rule. Like the old Jewish synagogues had their elders, every new church was to have its elders also. These synagogue elders are the men who, in some New Testament passages, are termed "rulers" of the synagogue. The sheep's well-being demanded them. Getting across this truth is the intention of verse 5. In every city there are to be elders.

Qualified Shepherds Are Essential

But notice the movement of thought now as we read on to verse 6 and following. It is not enough that the church have elders in name. They must have elders who are *qualified.* This being obvious, Paul gives some suggested qualifications. They are to be family men so that with this experience they can take care of the larger family of God. They are neither to be strikers nor brawlers, lest their board meetings be fusses and fights instead of constructive hours of prayer and planning. A church must not pick self-willed men, but gentlemen of self-control. To pass by that qualification will result in nothing but faction and friction. The congregations need elders who are "welders"—gentle, kind men who lead the sheep by example and inspiration. They do not need dictators who try to drive the flock where they do not wish to go.

Functioning, Qualified Shepherds Are Essential

When we read from Titus 1, starting at verse 10, we find that a church can have elders. We learn that these must be qualified shepherds in every way. But we further discover that if they do not *function* at their task of overseeing the flock, what profit is it? "There are many unruly men, vain talkers and deceivers, specially they of the circumcision [that is the Judaizers], whose mouths must be stopped." By whom? By the elders. They may be qualified, but what if they do not function?

The false teachers are overthrowing "whole houses," writes Paul. The early church did not meet in church buildings or elaborate tents. They met in homes, like the house of Priscilla and Aquilla, or that of Philemon, for example. If entire congregations were being converted from New Testament apostolic truth at the inroads of all kinds of heresy, something must be done. In the era of the New Testament some people went by subjective feeling, like the embryonic-gnostic, Cerinthus. Other people went after some false revelation brought by a charismatic. Other people went after Judaizers who clung too heavily upon the laws of the Old Testament revelation. How were the young sheep to distinguish which fodder was for them? Sheep would not know the difference perfectly. Only wise shepherds could know the good from the bad.

Do you know of a church that has elders—qualified elders—and yet has some trouble? Probably it is because they either do not know how, or are not willing, to stop the mouths of men who begin mixing into their teaching some erroneous and fatal doctrine! With tears, Paul had warned the Ephesian elders about wolves to arise among them, not sparing the flock (Acts 20:29-31). He knew by bitter experience what others have learned too late: A little wolf can scatter a great big flock of sheep. Every church needs *qualified elders who function.* Pastoring God's people is the greatest work in the world. Get qualified. Seek the good work of an overseer (1 Timothy 3:1). Function to the glory of God and the benefit of His dear people.

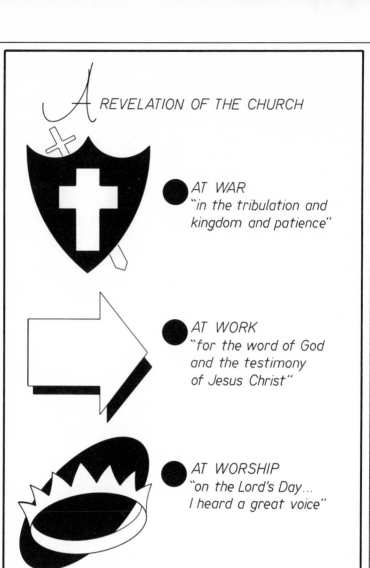

A REVELATION OF THE CHURCH

- AT WAR
  "in the tribulation and
  kingdom and patience"

- AT WORK
  "for the word of God
  and the testimony
  of Jesus Christ"

- AT WORSHIP
  "on the Lord's Day...
  I heard a great voice"

Chart Number 17

17 / revelation

In this chapter we are seeking for "the revelation in the *Revelation*." We are asking "What is the apocalypse in the *Apocalypse?*" I think you know that the Greek word *apokalupsis* is translated "revelation." It carries the idea of pulling back a curtain to reveal what had been hidden from view. When Jesus gives this revelation to John to pass on to us, what is it He wants us to see? The book is a revelation from Christ. But, also, it is both a revelation of Christ and of the church of Christ. The church is revealed AT WAR, AT WORK and AT WORSHIP (Chart #17). With this background, I invite you to look with me at yourself—Christ's church.

The Church at War

What are the revelations in Revelation regarding *the church at war?* We will begin at this point, because whoever sets out to follow the crucified Christ must not expect to get by without also bearing a cross. We are Christian soldiers. There is a battle going on. The world and the devil resist our message. They will try to stop us with all the artillery they have. We are going to have to face struggle, conflict, and suffering. Yet, in the end, know that we will have certain and eternal victory.

Open your Bible to the book of Revelation. Look at chapter 1, carefully reading verses 9 and 10. After the wonderful introduction of verses 1 through 8, we will find the purpose of John stated. He suggests there the three ideas upon which we are going to build. First read the words, "I John, your brother and partaker with you in the tribulation." Christ never did ask us to go where He had not gone, nor into a situation where He would not be with us. He knew opposition, suffering, and tribulation. His apostles never did write a letter to encourage a church until those apostles had been in the same kind of struggle, conflict, or difficulty. In this letter, John writes that, in spirit, he is with these churches in Asia (Smyrna, Thyatira, Pergamum, Laodicea, *etc.*). He knows what it is to be in tribulation. He knows that warfare is going on.

I assure you, this "tribulation" of verse 9 is not a tribulation of "three and one-half years," as in some premillenial theory. It is rather a representation of conditions for the entire Christian era. There will be trouble for God's people in this present evil world. There may be a "sea of glass" around the throne of God. Up in the heavens above, everything may be calm. But, here on earth, often the sea will be in turmoil, the wind blowing, the waves high.

Actually, apocalyptic literature was very common in the time that John wrote. Today, we are not well acquainted with it. For this reason we have had all kinds of trouble trying to understand this book that concludes our Bible. But we need to realize that the church of John's time was used to apocalyptic literature. They knew how to understand the book John wrote to them. Likely he had expounded and explained the books of Daniel and Ezekiel to his churches. Many men in the first century had written literature of this *genre.* Yet to our day but one example of it has come into our New Testament. It is a characteristic of all apocalyptic literature that there is a battle pictured between the opposing forces of light and darkness, good and evil, Heaven and Hell.

John is a "brother and partaker" with the recipients of his letter "in the tribulation and kingdom." It is because of the very fact that they are the citizens of the kingdom of Heaven that they are in the tribulation mentioned. Once you have entered into God's kingdom you are arrayed in spiritual armor. You are equipped with the shield of faith and the sword of the Spirit. From the beginning of your Christian life you face an enemy, and that enemy is real. On the canvas of Revelation, the apostle paints the devil with horrid and horrifying heads—seven of them. He has ten horns. And joining him in the battle against God's people are beasts and demons and locusts that come out of the pit of the abyss.

We read further, "I, John, your brother" am a "partaker with you in the tribulation and kingdom and patience." The last word means steadfastness. This is the virtue you and I must have if we are going to endure the very real opposition of a very real enemy. Luke 9:51 says that Jesus "steadfastly set his face to go to Jerusalem." You must steadfastly set your face

to go to death, if need be, for your convictions. Revelation
suggests so. You are a soldier of the cross.

The Church at Work

Read the next line of verse nine. "I . . . was in the isle that is
called Patmos, for the word of God and the testimony of
Jesus." These last phrases do not mean that John had gone
to this island to carry out an evangelistic program, although I
am sure that he tried to evangelize while he was there. The
fact is, he was put on this island to get him away from Asia
where he had been evangelizing so effectively. John's example clarifies his understanding that to make and develop
Christians is the *work of the Christian church.* It is the only
work Christ left to us. The Great Commission (Matthew
28:18-20) contains no order except to disciple the nations by
baptizing them, and to follow this by teaching the observation
of Christ's every command.

I sometimes ask my students at college if they can give me
an answer to these two questions: First, "Why did John write
his Gospel?" The second question is, "Why did John write the
book of Revelation?" I say in advance, "I know you are going
to give me one wrong answer and one right answer." To the
first question about the reason for John's Gospel, the students quote John 20:31, "That ye may believe that Jesus is the
Christ, the Son of God." In other words, the Gospel was written with an evangelistic purpose in mind. Its aim was to bring
people to faith and keep them in faith. But the same pupils do
not see at first why John wrote the last book of the New
Testament. The aim of Revelation was to keep the church
evangelizing. The dragon with seven heads and ten horns was
growling against that weak and comparatively small church.
When we see the church being threatened by as mighty a
force as pagan Rome, we wonder if the church possibly can
prevail. The answer Revelation reveals is that the dragon will
go down. The church will prevail. To what shall we attribute
the victory? The Lamb will overcome the dragon.

You already knew that the last book of the New Testament
ended with the evangelistic invitation: "The Spirit and the
bride say, Come. And he that heareth, let him say, Come. And
he that is athirst, let him come: he that will, let him take the

water of life freely." Is it too much to suggest that a book that ends with evangelistic concern might be expected to begin and continue with that same motive? If Revelation 22:17 is an evangelistic invitation, what is Revelation 1:9? Here, John simply and clearly states that he was put in isolation on the Isle of Patmos because he had been evangelizing and the government was trying to stop his mouth. The life-situation out of which this letter comes is a church doing its evangelizing, while a powerful State is saying, "Stop in the name of the law! Propagation of the Christian faith is no longer legal. It is illicit from now on." John writes to say, "Even when that dragon snarls, and the State says, 'No more preaching!' don't forget your higher orders of the Great Commission. Go into the world and keep preaching! Know that your truth will prevail. The kingdom of God will stand. The kingdoms of this world will go down." It is evident that you have the church at war because you have the church at its work of evangelism.

The Church at Worship

In Revelation we also want to see revealed *the church at worship* on the Lord's Day. "I was in the Spirit on the Lord's Day" is the wording of verse 10. Justin Martyr, Irenaeus, Ignatius, and other early churchmen used the phrase "the Lord's day" to refer to Sunday, the first day of the week. Our apostle is separated from his people in Asia by the Aegean Sea. He is very lonesome for he cannot be with his flock who are gathered on the mainland in worship. Yet, John becomes aware that he is not alone. The same Christ who is with those churches in Asia is also with John on Patmos. This fact becomes obvious as he hears a voice. It is a voice like that of many waters. It is a voice brilliant and clear like a trumpet sounding forth. John turns around to see the source. His eyes fall on none other than Jesus Christ there in living presence.

The church today gathers on the same resurrection day— the first day of the week—"the Lord's day." The believers gather around the table to commune. They always know that the living Lord, though invisible, is present. They are aware that as they hear the voice of the pulpit, it represents this voice of Christ. When the "word of Christ" is so heard, hope comes and courage comes and evangelism continues.

As we are prepared now to enter more deeply into the unique book of John, hear the call to arms, the call to evangelize, and the call to worship. Listen for anthems being sung and prayers being offered by the twenty-four elders. Seek to hear with your heart the angel choir and the singing congregation composed of redeemed men from every nation. Let fall upon the ears of your spirit the benedictions and the blessings. And before you leave this chapel of praise and before you hear the final chime of the closing verse, get on your knees. Join the great and last apostle prostrate before the King. Lay your crown before him who is Lord of lords.

ENEMY AGENTS

PERSECUTOR *(Pagan Government)*
PRIEST *(Pagan Religion)*
PROSTITUTE *(Pagan Morals)*

REVEALING
THE **CHURCH** AT
WAR

CHRIST'S ARMY

PREPARED *for Conflict*
PROVEN *by Suffering*
PRIMED *to Victory*

Chart Number 18

18 / the church at war

In a slightly more extensive way we now are ready to look three ways at the book of Revelation: First, the church *at war,* then *at work,* and finally *at worship.* We have remarked already that apocalyptic literature has the mark of conflict between two forces. We need to clarify that Christian apocalyptic literature (Revelation) and Jewish apocalyptic literature (Daniel and Ezekiel) are not totally like their counterparts in Babylonian and pagan literature. There you have two eternal forces in everlasting struggle. In Biblical apocalyptic literature there are two forces in conflict and the conflict lasts throughout history, but one force is not eternal. Light will last endlessly. Darkness will not prevail. At the close of the book we are now studying, the impure woman—the harlot—is gone for good. The pure bride of Christ remains forever. At the conclusion of Revelation, the Holy City is there, never to be destroyed; but the city of Babylon "is fallen," never to rise again. Satan is a created being. He is not an eternal being. He had a beginning. He will have an end.

This awareness prepares us to understand that the future is guaranteed, predestined by God. Righteousness will win out. Iniquity will die out. Truth and right are going to win. There is no question about that. This is Scriptural predestination. There is nothing man can do to stop Christ's march. There is nothing the devil can do, nothing all the imps of Hell can do. No power can stop God from fulfilling His promises. He is going to redeem all who believe and obey His Son. That is predetermined. Nothing will ever change that.

Persecutor–Pagan Government

In the warfare described in Revelation there is a dragon with seven heads and ten horns. You meet this enemy in several places. For instance, take chapter 12. There this snarling dragon is called the "great red dragon." His seven heads represent the seven hills of Rome. The frightening dragon has water like a river about to flood from his mouth to drown the woman. Satanic forces are about to engulf all the work of the kingdom of God.

In chapter 13 and again in chapter 17, we meet other beings who side with the devil. This fallen angel, this Satan, has evil helpers and corrupted "agents." The first one I label as a *persecutor*, the second as a *priest*, the third as a *prostitute* (Chart #18). One beast rises from the sea and one rises from the land. Both are helpers of this dragon. If the dragon is the devil—the serpent, the one that deceives mankind—who are his helpers? When in Revelation 13:1-8, the first beast rises from the sea, you recognize a composite of Daniel's four beasts that came likewise from the sea. I take this first beast imagery to mean that the devil is going to use *pagan government*–pagan legislation—to try to restrict the church in its work of evangelism. The church is going to have to war sometimes with the non-Christian systems of government. The devil, the invisible dragon, is going to work through a very visible entity, rising on the world scene. There is worldly civil government on the one hand. But there is more than that.

Priest–Pagan Religion

From the land there also will come another beast. It, too, will be endowed with "seven heads and ten horns." Does this not indicate that the dragon will use more than pagan government? Will he not work also through *pagan religion?* The latter part of chapter 13 (verses 10 through 18) describes this second beast from the land. We note that this beast makes an image for people to fall down and worship. He tries to get all the people to worship both the dragon and the first beast. Thus it appears that this awesome power is a religious entity. At least, in the experiences of Christian history from A.D. 96 to our day, only sometimes is the opposition to the church a non-Christian government. At other times it is a non-Christian religion. Back then there was pagan Rome and there was religious Rome. The second worked on the people to move them to bow down to the government.

In our modern day, right here and now, it is possible for people to go around the world to spread "Americanism" or "Socialism" or "Communism" rather than Christianity. Sometimes even good government can become an idol that men begin to worship and put first in their lives. Satan has been known to use all kinds of forms and forces in his efforts to bring men to destruction. He starts out to be a persecutor and that is pagan government. He then tries to get religion to cause people to bow down and to do as a religous act whatever the emperor says to do.

Prostitute–Pagan Morals

At chapter 17 you meet once again "seven heads and ten horns." But this time you find a gaudy woman dressed in red. She has rings upon her fingers. She is very, very attractive—very, very seductive. She is called a harlot and the mother of harlots. She is another agent of this invisible one known as the devil, or Satan. When the enemy of the soul does not destroy the church by legalistic restrictions, when he does not do it through some pagan religion, he strives to bring the church down through the kind of morality that is called the "new morality." At Satan's suggestion the standards of the world, rather than the revealed standards of God, are made to sound right to people. Note the seduction here in chapter 17—the lure from holiness to iniquity. Note it well for history has repeated itself and will continue to repeat itself until the end of time. While the world stands, we always will have these evil forces in the various forms of human government, religion, and morality.

Prepared for Conflict

But we are not in Satan's army. We are in Christ's brigade. Whoever fights in the army of God had better put on the whole armor so he can stand in the evil day. Satan knows how to tear people down. He is cunning in his efforts to conquer God's forces. At all times the Christian soldier had better be at his defensive best, as well as on his offensive best.

From Genesis 3:15 throughout the entire Scriptures, you find reflected the opposition against which believers must contend. There will be conflict and suffering, but also victory. In Revelation you meet the soldiers of the cross *prepared for the conflict.* You discover them *proven by suffering* amid the great tribulation. But you see them *primed to victory,* anticipating certain success.

If the Lamb of God had to die, if there was a cross for Jesus, there will be a cross for every Christian. And you and I will be better prepared for the kind of life we have to meet out there, if we know these facts from the beginning. If the Master suffered, the servants of the Master are going to suffer. They are going to have conflict. Therefore, John started out in chapter 1, "I John, your brother and partaker with you in the tribulation" (Revelation 1:9). We have the CHURCH AT WAR. The entire kingdom age is the age of tribulation. While we are in the world, the storms rage, the ocean rises and swells, the tide goes in and out, and there is a whipping of doctrinal winds. But Jesus has said, "In the world ye have tribulation: but be of good cheer; I have overcome the world" (John 16:33). Being forewarned of tribulation, we can be forearmed. A man can be prepared for conflict, if he knows it is going to be there.

If you, personally, came into Christianity thinking things were going to be easy, you have been disappointed already. But if you expected trouble, if you knew there was going to be hardship, if you understood you would need to win battles, you were prepared. In the war for right every good soldier of the cross expects to contend for the faith. Every such servant of God needs to be aware that to lose some battles is not to lose the war. That very preparation is a major step toward victory.

Proven by Suffering

Revelation further clarifies the truth that we are *proven by suffering* that we undergo. All along life's way we may face suffering and sacrifice. We may be cast to the lions. We, like Paul, may be driven out of town, stoned, and left for dead. Yet, we can know that, while we are proven by suffering, we are being *primed to victory*. Babylon fell. Medo-Persia fell. Rome fell. But the church will never fall. The gates of death will not prevail against Christ's church. Expect victory and get on the victory side!

Primed to Victory

The most optimistic book in all the world is the book of Revelation. Read about the "sword" held in the mouth of the one called the *Logos* or the "Word of God." Chapter 19 tells about a battle going on with one army dressed in white. These soldiers are following this "Word of God" who is riding upon a white horse. Here, again, is conflict which you recognize. You see yourself in Christ's army fighting against all the degrading forces of pagan government, pagan religion, and pagan morality. You know that in such a battle there has to be conflict and there is going to be suffering. But, in the heat of this battle, you sense there is going to be victory. And, as a Christian, you are prepared for the conflict. You have put on the whole armor of God. And you have the commander's guarantee that after the suffering there will be total victory. Revelation 11:15 pulled back the curtain long enough to show you the kingdoms of the world becoming the kingdom of our Lord and His Christ. There you behold King Jesus, reigning forever and ever.

In chapter 20, by a change in symbol, we meet the devil in the abyss for a thousand years. He is bound tight by a great chain. Like Paul the earlier prisoner in Rome, John the prisoner on Patmos knows that he is really the free person. The evil forces are the defeated ones and down they will topple. All Biblical prophecy shows the struggle of righteousness against iniquity, but God's church ultimately prevails. Always the other kingdoms fall. Keep that in mind and it will keep you in the battlefront.

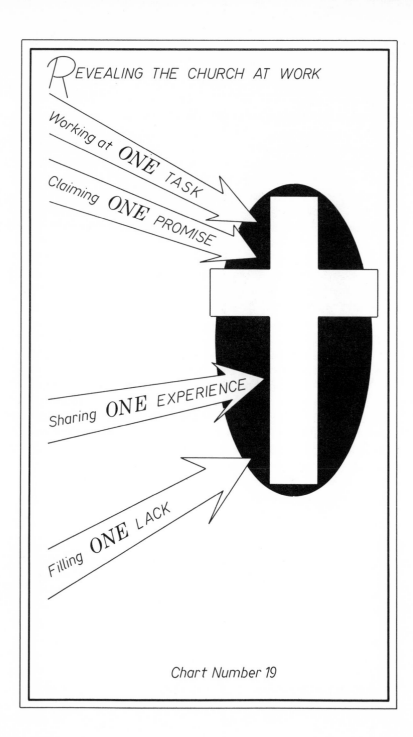

Revealing the church at work

Working at ONE TASK

Claiming ONE PROMISE

Sharing ONE EXPERIENCE

Filling ONE LACK

Chart Number 19

19 / the church at work

We search in Revelation for more revelation. What else is revealed in the book that pulls back the curtain, showing the future? The first revelation we have seen is that we are in God's army, at conflict with evil. We are made aware that we must face suffering in this world. Only in God's Heaven will there be peace and calmness and a "sea of glass." Here, there will be great tribulation. When we go to "the land beyond the river," we will be dressed in white robes because our garments have been cleansed by the blood of the lamb. There, all will know that we have come out of a world where there has been little but tribulation for the saints of God.

As we press our search for further truth, hear once again the words of John. But this time listen longer than before: "I John, your brother and partaker with you in the tribulation and kingdom and patience which are in Jesus, was in the isle that is called Patmos, for the Word of God and the testimony of Jesus." The conflict and battle we have just discussed has been intensified by our divine work. We were assigned by our great Commander to go into all the world and preach the gospel, to disciple the nations, to baptize, and to win people from every kindred, tribe, tongue, and nation. This is likewise the church's one work as revealed in Revelation (Chart #19).

Working at One Task

Starting at chapter 1, notice throughout the book the symbols by which the church is pictured. Revelation is unrolled by symbols and signs. Revelation 1:1 indicates that the message was "signified" (*sign*-ified) unto the apostle John. One might say that this is a divine warning to human interpreters not to take the book literally, but to understand it symbolically. Just as you always read history as history and law as law, you need to treat apocalyptic literature as apocalyptic literature. If you allegorize law you will come to all sorts of erroneous conclusions. Or, if you take historical, actual and factual material, and handle it as symbolism, you will misun-

111

derstand that, too. So take this writing as it was intended. It was meant to be interpreted symbolically.

Look at Revelation as a book of pictures or as a great mural. Seek to find the church described in relation to its task. The figures found are varied. But even though they are so different in symbol they all are representing the very one truth. It is the reality that the CHURCH AT WORK is an evangelistic agency. If I might paraphrase Thomas Campbell's "The church of Christ on earth is essentially, intentionally, and constitutionally one," I would go on. I would add, "The church of Christ on earth is essentially, intentionally, and constitutionally one missionary society." An "evangelistic agency" is all the church at work is meant to be.

As you are looking through chapter 1 to discover how the church is symbolized there, you note that in each of these seven communities of Asia there is a lampstand (or in the King James Version—a candlestick). Now apply that observation. A candle is one thing, a candlestick is something else. A candlestick functions in upholding the candle. A lamp is the light. The lampstand is that which upholds the light. Application? The church in Laodicea or Los Angeles, Thyatira or Trenton, is to be that agency which upholds the light of Christ's gospel in its darkened community. The goal of every church is to uphold its message. It is to shine in its blackened surroundings, for ignorance is there, and iniquity is there, and darkness is there. The job of the church is to let God's light shine—not to place that light under a bushel, but to let the lamp give out its brightness.

Someone has said that in the church we have two kinds of members. They are the "pillars" and the "caterpillars." The pillars support the work of the church and the caterpillars just go in and out occasionally. First Timothy 3:15, 16 looks at the church in a way similar to Revelation 1—3. There Paul speaks of "the church of the living God" as "the pillar and ground of the truth." He then lists six important facts regarding the gospel, supported by the church as pillar and ground. He uses the words of an early Christian hymn. Our mission, or work, as revealed by John, is the same. God's people are to be that supporting agency that upholds Jesus and dispels the darkness of ignorance and the blackness of iniquity.

For a totally different symbol of the church, take a look at Revelation 12 which describes the church as Jesus' bride, much as does Revelation 21:9. Here is pictured a woman who, I believe, portrays the bride of Christ, the church. She has twelve stars around her head, representing the twelve apostles, the leaders of the church. She is standing on the moon. The moon reigns over the darkness, as the sun reigns over the day. And since to stand upon something shows it to be subdued—conquered, subjected—this picture is that of the church overcoming the realm of darkness. It is important to observe that this woman is pregnant. She is about to bear a child. Or, we could say she is about to have another convert. Out in front of her is this dragon with seven heads and ten horns. He is snarling away, trying to destroy the church and the converts of that church as they come forth. A flood of water is seen to come out of his mouth. The flood is intended to drown those who are called the children of God who "keep the commandments of God, and hold the testimony of Jesus" (Revelation 12:17).

You see that we have jumped from a candlestick to a woman about to have a child. It may be gaining clarity in your mind that the images, while different, uphold the same truth about the church. The church is in this world to do an evangelistic task.

In yet another place in the book (Revelation 5:10), the church is pictured as a kingdom of priests. It is a kingdom in which every citizen is a priest. If you ask, "What is the sacrifice New Testament priests offer to their God?" recall Paul's "offering up of the Gentiles" (Romans 15:16) or the Hebrew writer's description of the sacrifice as "the fruit of lips which make confession to his name" (Hebrews 13:15). Lampstand—bride—priests offering sacrifice—are varied symbols that tell one story. The church has ONE TASK—to win the world and fulfill the ascending Lord's commission.

Claiming One Promise

What is the *one promise* from which we can gain the strength to do our *one task?* I invite you again to cast your eyes upon the book of Revelation. Search now in chapters 1, 2, and 3 asking, "Where is Jesus?" When you find the verses where the church is pictured by a lampstand, ask, "Where is Christ in relationship to these light-bearing communities?" Is He far away, up in the sky? No! He is right down here with them in the tribulation— in the conflict. He is by the side of His workers in the world. He is to be seen walking "in the midst of the candlesticks" (Revelation 1:13).

Observe that there is a promise connected with the Great Commission to disciple the nations (Matthew 28:19, 20). It is "Lo, I am with you always." Tie the command and its promise together. When the Great Commission is being obeyed by Christ's servants, they are not to forget He is with them. The book of Revelation is a picture book to show us that Jesus' promise is the truth in fact. Christ is with the church in the struggle. He is with the church as it upholds the light. His presence is not far away. Therefore hear this assurance of strength and cling to it.

Now continue to chapter 4 where John, in the first verse, is raptured into Heaven. This is to give him the vantage point of Heaven. Without that he will not see what is happening to Jesus' disciples from the Father's heavenly perspective. If a Christian has to struggle down here on earth against the enemy, the devil, at least let him see God's hand in it all. Thus John goes into Heaven at the beginning of chapter 4. But before John looks down from Heaven to see things from that different angle, through chapters 4 and 5, he looks around in Heaven itself. What does he find but a throne. And after his difficult Patmos experience, John perhaps is surprised at what he now sees. On the throne is no less than God, himself. There are also round about God twenty-four elders and four living creatures. They are praising Him as creator of Heaven and earth. In the second of these two chapters, you find a Lamb in joint-reign with the Creator. Here, the songs of chapter 4 on "creation" turn to songs of "redemption." Not only is the Father being worshiped, the Son is being praised also.

Now let us analyze what Revelation is indicating by all this. If the church is symbolized as a light-bearing institution, we desire to ask with what success it will carry out this light-spreading ministry. When you get caught up into Heaven with John, you find that God is on the throne. It is not Domitian, not Nero, not Hitler. It is not even the Communists. You thus conclude, that after all appearances to the contrary, God is still running things. So whenever you get tempted to believe that, in the evangelistic program in your local church, you are not going to be successful, read the refreshing book of Revelation. Not only is there revelation of "working at the one task" of soul winning, there is the revelation of our "claiming the one promise" that we are going to win the world because God is still on the throne.

Further, notice in Revelation 5:1 that a book is in the hand of God on the throne. And what is this book? It is the book of the future. But it is said to be closed with seven seals. Seven is the number of totality (seven days in a week, seven colors in a spectrum, seven notes in a scale). Here seven means completeness. Therefore, if the book of the future has seven seals on it, that means the future is totally sealed. Nobody, but nobody, among God's creatures knows about tomorrow.

Even though that is true, look where the book of the future is. It is in God's hands! Now that is another assuring promise! Promise one: Christ is with the church. Don't worry. Promise two: God is on the throne. Don't worry. Promise three: The future is in God's hands. Don't you worry! Keep in there! Fight the battle! In this struggle—this war—"The weapons of our warfare are . . . mighty before God to the casting down of strongholds" (2 Corinthians 10:4). Put on the whole armor of God and work at this one task.

The promise that God is reigning and holds the future is encouraging! But John still is concerned. Christians are suffering. By now all the other apostles are dead. He alone lives, and he is on an island as a slave. What is tomorrow going to bring for the church? In chapter 5 it says John scoured the Heaven, the earth, and under the earth, but he found no being worthy to open the book of the future.

At this point the record says that John began to weep much. It reminds me of an optometrist in Milwaukie, Oregon, named Dr. Donald Chambers, who says, "You can't be optimistic if you have a misty optic." John's misty optics are working. He's weeping. Why? Because no one is found worthy to open the book of the future. And then an elder, one of the twenty-four, calls on John to look to the Lion. John turns and there is to be seen a lion that looks like a lamb that has "been slain" but now is "standing." That imagery pictures a full-gospel revelation. He, who has been the Lamb of God (Jesus Christ) and slain for our sins, is now resurrected and standing once again. And the One that you would call God's lamb of sacrifice is also the Lion of the tribe of Judah. He is the acknowledged King of kings and the Lord of lords. He is worthy to open the book of the future.

Here we ask once again, "What is this book revealing about the work of the church, which is evangelism?" We who go forth bearing the light of Christ find that the God who gave the charge is still on the throne. We discover that the book of the future, though unknown to human minds, is in His hand. We next see that when Jesus Christ speaks (chapter 6) things begin to happen under His control.

Suppose you were a gambling man. Imagine that millenniums ago you were going to gamble between the dinosaurs and the rabbits. Pretend that you had to prejudge who would be the greatest and live on and on and on. There were the big, powerful, mighty dinosaurs on the one hand. On the other hand there were but the "li'l ol' rabbits." You probably would have lost with me and voted on the dinosaurs. Now, look at the rabbits! There are no dinosaurs. The meek do inherit the earth. In the future, Jesus is in control, not the seemingly mighty men.

More good news is found in chapter 7. There we meet the "one hundred and forty and four thousand" from the twelve tribes. In chapter 14, once again this same group is mentioned. You will find that our Jehovah's Witness friends are in error. This number does not refer to the entire number that are going to be in Heaven. Revelation simply is suggesting that these are the "firstfruits" (Revelation 14:4). You may know that in the Old Testament days a farmer plowed his field, planted it, and waited for the crop. When the harvest time first came, he would take just a swath from the corner of the field. This he would wave before the Lord. This became known as the "wave offering" and "the offering of the firstfruit" (Leviticus 23:9-11). That little swath in the corner does not represent all the redeemed going into the garner of Heaven. Rather, it pictures just the "first" swath.

When the church initially began among the Jews on the Day

of Pentecost, it commenced with twelve Jewish apostles. There were added on that glorious day "three thousand" more Jews. Soon the number grew until Luke's book of Acts records that they could not even number them. Luke explains that even a great host of priests became obedient to the faith (Acts 6:7). By the time John writes in A.D. 96 there is a "first swath" from the twelve tribes numbered figuratively at one hundred and forty-four thousand. This is a symbolic number for a great host of redeemed people "out of every tribe of the children of Israel" (Revelation 7:4). But see the rest of it. If that is but the firstfruit, what is to follow? The Scripture continues that then there came "a great multitude, which no man could number, out of every nation and of all tribes and peoples and tongues" (Revelation 7:9). There are so many people redeemed that they are an innumerable host.

We are reading a book called an "apocalypse" with its concept of the pulling back of a curtain. As the curtain has drawn back, we have seen the church at warfare, in struggle with the devil himself. We have seen the church at work doing its one divine assignment. And we are learning that while we are working at the one task, we can claim the ONE PROMISE, "Lo, I am with you always even unto the end of the age." By the end of the story (Revelation 21, 22), Heaven will be here. God will be tabernacled among His people. Satan will be bound in a bottomless pit (Revelation 20). He will be cast into a lake of fire. While Babylon will be gone, the new Jerusalem will remain. While the harlot will be heard of no more, the church will be with Christ for ever and ever.

Sharing One Experience

One task has been revealed in the book before us. *One promise* has been given for the church to claim. It may be phrased: "Christ died for a lost world. He did not die for a lost cause." The *one experience* which we have all shared is our next truth to realize. Revelation 1:5, 6, for example, says, "[He] loveth us, and loosed us from our sins by his blood; and he made us to be a kingdom, to be priests unto his God and Father." As we, the church, begin to read this letter, we know that it is we who are recipients of God's love. We already have been reached evangelistically. Since salvation's torch has been passed on to us, it become a recognized responsibility that we must pass it on to others. This is the ONE common EXPERIENCE every Christian has had. He has been evangelized. He has been converted. Therefore, he will share his experience with others. He will hand the truth of salvation on. Being reached by the saving message was an experience enjoyed by every initial recipient of this last book of the Bible. Every reader from Ephesus, Pergamum, Thyatira, Sardis, and beyond had been redeemed by the blood of Jesus Christ. He had experienced coming to faith and baptism. That experience made him debtor to others.

Again, Revelation 12:11 tells us that Satan was overcome "because of the blood of the Lamb, and because of the word of their testimony; and they loved not their life even unto death." Here the devil's defeat is attributed both to Christ's death and to the fact that testimony was borne to this event. Further, when the witnesses were hampered by a threatening government, they went on talking, loving not their lives even unto their deaths. This courage to witness proved, once again, that they had enjoyed the "one experience" of being evangelized. Now they were set to bring that Evangel to others. Those with names in the Lamb's book of life are anxious to enroll many more.

Filling One Lack

We recapitulate for clarity. Revealed in Revelation is our work. We have one *task*. It is to evangelize. Revealed in Revelation regarding that work is the *promise* that we are going to have evangelistic success. Revealed in Revelation is the evident truth that the present converters earlier were converted. Each had the same *experience* of being evangelized. There is one final thought revealed in Revelation about the Church's mission. It has to do with *filling the one lack.*

What is the one lack? I believe I know what it is today. I think I see what it has been for the two thousand years since John's day. I see that some first-generation Christians received the gospel. I observe that they settled down contentedly. They did not keep spreading the message around their world hopefully, excitedly, and urgently. The ONE LACK Jesus pointed to was that they had lost their "first love"

(Revelation 2:4). They had become "lukewarm" about the work of saving the unsaved (Revelation 3:16). They were doing their Christian service through stagnant routine, through cold obligation, through dull sense of duty. They were not doing their ministries spontaneously, joyously, lovingly. They lost their drive and passion to share their faith. Someone said that Jesus often treated people as if their lives were islands. That is, when He first met them, He seemingly would sail around them until He found their difficulty. He wanted to be helpful. So when He found their real problem, then and there He would "land." If Christ finds a woman at some well whose problem is home life, He might be expected to land on the marriage question. When He comes upon a rich young ruler whose problem is greed, He likely will come to port on the money question. This point is to make us ask a practical question. If Jesus should stand in the pulpit of your local church building this week, knowing that He wanted to be helpful, where do you think He would land? Under the loving eye of Christ, a youthful man of power and wealth was diagnosed, "One thing thou lackest." The remedy was, "Sell all that thou hast, and distribute unto the poor" (Luke 18:22). Could our lack be soul winning? Could our cure be giving the rich gospel to the spiritually poor and lost all about us?

If I said our present lack was evangelism, you might reply that evangelism is all you talk about at your church. Right! And there is just the trouble. You and I *talk* more about soul winning than we *do* soul winning. At the present hour across the U.S.A., Sunday-school classes regularly talk about evangelism. Churches have continual conferences on evangelism. These activities, while good in themselves, are poor substitutes for actual evangelism. At a national brotherhood convention, a voice from the podium may inquire, "How many here are preachers?" At the question most every ordained person on some church's payroll immediately would raise his hand. Then and there you might feel the urge to say, "Now wait a minute. There is a difference between preaching and teaching. 'Preaching' is telling good news to non-Christians. 'Teaching' is instructing the gathered disciples of Christ in the implications and meaning of that gospel. Are you really all preachers?" We are possibly in error calling the Sunday-morning pulpit lesson, preaching. Speaking precisely, that is not preaching. That is teaching those who are already believers to obey the Word of the Lord more perfectly. A man may call himself a preacher or an evangelist, but he is not one in fact unless he is talking the good news to non-Christians.

I conclude that the one thing we lack is to remember to do our mission. We talk about evangelism all the time. We regularly schedule evangelistic meetings where we talk to each other. We even get a few outsiders to come out to the services and hear us talk about it. But this has but little to do with true evangelism. The one thing we lack is the one thing the Great Commission assigns in the word, "Go!" Our Lord nowhere commands non-believing people, "come to church." He orders believing disciples to "go into all the world." This demands that sometime, somewhere, and somehow you and I get outside the fellowship hall where Christians meet and into non-Christian groups where lost men gather.

As I write this book I recognize that I am not preaching. As I speak to the churches on the Lord's Day, I am not preaching. Again, I rather am teaching disciples of Jesus Christ. Feeding God's flock is a part of our ministry. But the one thing we lack is, we do not preach much any more. We do not encounter the non-Christians often enough.

C. H. Dodd has a book called *Apostolic Preaching.* Alexander Campbell, who preceded him by many years, agreed that preaching is one thing as distinctive from teaching as baptizing is distinctive from teaching. Preaching is addressing a non-Christian with the gospel about Christ. Preaching is announcing news to a man who has not known it. This being true, I wish every "preacher" would examine his daytime schedule. He needs to check on himself and see how much time he has allotted to approaching non-members.

We who are not ordained preachers need to look at our Sunday-school classes, church gatherings, and conventions where we talk about evangelism. Talking to ourselves about evangelism is a necessary preparation, but it is not doing the work of evangelism. You only are evangelizing when you talk to a wife, a neighbor, a business partner, a schoolmate, a brother, or someone else outside the church about Christ's claim upon his life.

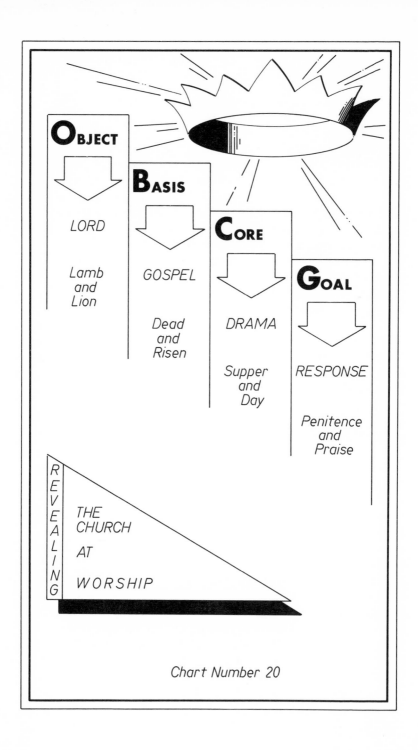

OBJECT

LORD

*Lamb
and
Lion*

BASIS

GOSPEL

*Dead
and
Risen*

CORE

DRAMA

*Supper
and
Day*

GOAL

RESPONSE

*Penitence
and
Praise*

REVEALING

*THE
CHURCH*

AT

WORSHIP

Chart Number 20

20 / the church at worship

I desire that you shift gears just now. Slow down your mind that has girded itself for battle and clothed itself for work. It is time for worship. Shall we be very quiet for the next few moments? In worshipful silence, join me as we now tiptoe into the last book of the Bible. When we go into this place to worship, at first we will not want to stay. This is because the Isle of Patmos is a barren and rocky place. As a matter of fact, what we hear does not sound good to our ears. It is a whip cracking upon the back of a slave. And what can we see down in the mines that is really inviting, making us want to look Godward? But I suggest to you that we tarry a little while. I say this because, as we walk through the chapel of the twenty-two chapters of Revelation, each chapter is going to become like a stained-glass window. We are going to be introduced to a symphony of sound and color like eye has never seen, nor ear heard, nor mind of man imagined concerning the wonders of Christian worship (Chart #20).

I want to welcome you to a worship service on the Isle of Patmos. I want to invite you to listen to angel choirs as they sing. There will be no church bells. Yet, there will be liturgical trumpets calling us both to bow the knee to God and to stand erect in the presence of sin, as we sing His praise.

It is "the Lord's Day." We have entered the liturgical setting of the apocalypse. We are reading the happiest book ever written. We are about to worship under the direction of John the Revelator.

It is our intention to take a look at this final book of the Scriptures as a document valid in the study of how the early Christians worshiped. Alexander Campbell felt that the church of his day should follow the church of New Testament days in its worship. So he gave us a hymn book in which he put five of his own hymns along with songs of others. One of Campbell's hymns was based on Revelation 19. Of importance to us now is that the middle portion of Campbell's

Psalms, Hymns and Spiritual Songs was patterned after the hymns in John's Revelation, which are songs to the praise of Christ.

We want to affirm four truths about the early liturgy that you find in the apocalypse. The first truth is that the object of worship in the New Testament church is the Lord Jesus. The second is that the basis of this worship is the fact of His death and resurrection. The third is that the core of this worship is the Lord's Supper and the Lord's Day—emblems of that death and resurrection. The fourth is that the goal of Christian worship is the human response of penitence and praise.

The Object of Worship

It must appear surprising that the Lord Jesus is the OBJECT *of Christian worship.* It is strange because the author of Revelation is a monotheist. John has been steeped in the Old Testament and the Ten Commandments given by Moses. Hear the primary command, "Thou shalt have no other gods before [besides] me." The second is like unto it, "Thou shalt not make unto thee a graven image." John knew that we must not only worship the true God, but we dare not worship the true God under false forms. Simon Peter, a companion of John, had the experience of having Cornelius fall at his feet to worship him. Peter cried, "Stand up; I myself also am a man" (Acts 10:26). Another co-worker of John is Paul, who at Lystra found people bringing garlands. These Lystrians scarcely could be constrained from worshiping Paul and Barnabas. But the missionaries asked why they did these things to men of like passions with themselves (Acts 14:15). You remember that Jesus, the Lord of John and Peter and Paul, had resisted the tempter in the wilderness with the words, "Get thee hence, Satan: for it is written, Thou shalt worship the Lord thy God, and him only shalt thou serve" (Matthew 4:10). In Revelation, John momentarily forgets he should worship only God, as he falls down at the feet of an angel. However, the angel quickly shouts, "See thou do it not: I am a fellowservant . . . worship God" (Revelation 22:9). So Revelation agrees that the only object of true worship is God who sits upon the throne.

Further, be cognizant that the life situation out of which this book comes is emperor worship. Christians will not bow the knee to a Caesar or to a city. Yet, while they will not bow down before dragon or demon, angel or apostle, empire or emperor, every Christian readily will bow the knee to Jesus Christ.

"Our Lord and God" is the title that history books say Domitian required everyone to use toward him in spoken worship. This emperor required his citizens to begin their address to him with the acclamation, "Worthy art thou our Lord and God, Domitian." In the light of this state demand, read Revelation 4:11. There the twenty-four elders say, "Worthy art thou, our Lord and our God." They do not, however, refer these words to Domitian but to the true God who made Heaven and earth. The object of worship in the church is He who sits upon the throne and the Lamb who shares that throne (Revelation 5:9, 12).

It is said in Revelation that the harlot sits on a beast of seven heads. This totalitarian state, reigning from the city of seven hills, has names of blasphemy written upon it. Caesars, such as Augustus, were ordering: "Call me Augustus" which means "worthy of worship." This is blasphemy to a Christian. There had been the man, Julius Caesar, who accepted the title "The Divine Julius." We all remember at an earlier time there had been in Syria, Antiochus Epiphanes, meaning Antiochus "God manifest." Believers in Jesus called such claims blasphemous.

Before there was emperor worship there was the worship of Rome personified. They called the city *Roma aeterna,* implying that Rome is the "eternal city." John likes to point out in this last book of the Bible that this "Babylon" is going to fall. She, which claims to be worthy of worship and to have the God-like quality of living forever, will die. The worshipers in Revelation have been faithful to Jesus Christ their Lord. They will not worship the goddess Rome nor call the emperor divine. They will say "Christ is Lord," but not "Caesar is Lord." They will keep themselves clean from such blasphemy. In contrast to the sacrilegious worship of the beast, in Revelation 14:7 they would worship God who "made the heaven and the earth and sea and fountains of waters."

The only object of worship in Revelation is the Lord. True

believers would not worship the demons (Revelation 9:20). These whose names were in the Lamb's book of life would not bow before the dragon. Disciples of Jesus Christ could not worship Satan any more than they could bow the knee to an angel or an apostle.

We are affirming that the early Christian church was that church which had as its object of worship only the Lord. The question now raised is, "If they will not bow to the demonic, and they refuse to bow to the human, and they even are forbidden to bow to the angelic, why will they then bow to Jesus?" It must be that He is more than just a man. It must be that He is not even a created angel. If Jesus accepts worship, then He must be what He claimed to be—divine!

I have heard all kinds of arguments pro and con as to the authorship of the Gospel of John, the Epistles of John, and the Revelation of John. The more time I spend studying liturgy, the more I am encouraged to stay with the conviction that one author is the writer of all. Modern New Testament scholars are discovering liturgy in the first Epistle of John, and they are recognizing liturgy in the Revelation of John. I remember a course in Johannine literature given by Frederick Shilling of U.S.C. He showed the Gospel of John to be filled with "eucharistic" (Lord's Supper) and "baptismal" understanding. Also look at the high Christology of these books. The Gospel of John begins, "In the beginning was the Word, and the Word was with God, and the Word was God." The entire book, written in the afterglow of Christ's resurrection, has its climactic summary verses in 20:30, 31. The final illustration before this affirmation of sonship is the instance of Thomas falling at the feet of Jesus, saying, "My Lord and my God"—the very same words recorded in Revelation and required by Domitian. The Epistles of John are directed against Cerinthus and docetic gnosticism. These had taken the apostolic testimony regarding Jesus and perverted it. They had asserted that Christ really did not become flesh. They changed and twisted the story about Jesus, the true Lord and God. And so the final statement of John's first Epistle is, "Little children, guard yourselves from idols," because any other Jesus than the one revealed in the apostolic word is a false god, an "idol."

The *Didache,* a book reflecting how the church worshiped around A.D. 100 to 125, has every prayer in it Christ centered (see 10:14 or 19:10). When Pliny the younger writes in A.D. 112 to Trajan who was then governor of Syria, he says that these Christians, when they worshiped, met "on a stated day and sang songs antiphonally to Christ as God." This agreed with what we find in Revelation. The worship of the ancient church was the worship of Jesus. The Lamb, who is also the Lion, is sharing the throne of his Father (Revelation 5:5, 6). The titles reserved for Jehovah in the Old Testament are applied to Jesus in this book. The things that only God can do are said here to be done by Jesus—things such as giving grace and peace, searching the hearts of men, or sitting upon the throne. When we finish a reading of Revelation, we have learned that, while one ought not to bow to the demonic, the angelic, or the human, every knee should bow and every tongue confess that Jesus Christ is Lord to the glory of God the Father. He is worthy to be worshiped (Revelation 5:12-14).

The Basis of Worship

If the reflected worship of the last book of the Bible is a worship of our Lord—Lion and Lamb—what is the justification for such worship? How can a rigid monotheist who says, "Worship only God," bow the knee to Jesus? What is the theological BASIS for this? There is only one answer. That answer is the gospel. *The Lamb slain has become the Lion risen to reign.* That is, the fact of Christ's death on the cross, followed by His resurrection from the grave, has declared Him to be what He always claimed to be, and what others called blasphemy. He claimed to be God incarnate. He was Emmanuel. He was God in human flesh.

First Timothy 3:15 says that the church is "pillar and ground of the truth." The truth that it upholds is then stated in the words of an early hymn of the church. The song is about Jesus as God "manifested in the flesh, justified in the spirit, seen of angels, preached among the nations, believed on in the world, received up in glory." What some scholars identify as another hymn (Philippians 2:6-8) reads in part: "Who, existing in the form of God, counted not the being on an equality with God a thing to be grasped, but emptied himself, taking the form of a servant." John 1:14 is right, "The Word became flesh, and dwelt among us." The hymn writer, William E. Booth-Clibborn, is right with his phrasing:

> Down from His glory, ever-living story,
> My God and Savior came, and Jesus was His name.
> Born in a manger, to His own a stranger,
> A man of sorrows, tears and agony.
>
> What condescension, bringing us redemption;
> That in the dead of night, not one faint hope in sight,
> God gracious, tender, laid aside His splendor,
> Stooping to woo, to win, to save my soul.[1]

What is the justification for bowing the knee to Jesus and not bowing the knee to angel or man? It is because of who Jesus is! First, He is the Lamb slain from the foundation of the world. This is the gospel. And thus you read in Revelation 1:5, He "loveth us, and loosed us from our sins by his blood." How do you beat the devil, the one who binds us in sin? Revelation 12:11 answers that the great dragon, the old serpent, the one called Satan, was overcome "because of the blood of the Lamb." Who are these on high that you see dressed in white robes? They are the ones who have "washed their robes, and made them white in the blood of the Lamb" (Revelation 7:14). To read Revelation is to read from one who, like Paul, could say, "I determined not to know anything among you, save Jesus Christ, and him crucified" (1 Corinthians 2:2).

There is another side to this coin. The gospel is not only that Jesus died for our sins, but that He rose again. And so the Lamb symbol turns to a Lion symbol. The lion is known as the king of the beasts. In Revelation it stands for the Lion of the tribe of Judah, the One who conquered death and now reigns forever. Jesus died. But He is Alpha and Omega, the beginning and the end. He is the one who can say, "I am the first and the last, and the Living one; and I was dead, and behold, I am alive for evermore" (Revelation 1:17, 18). Did you think He still was in a tomb outside the city of Jerusalem? No! He is walking in A.D. 96 right in the midst of the lampstands and will be doing so in A.D. 1996. The very hope of the return of Christ is simply the fruit of faith in the resurrection of Christ.

---

[1]Copyright 1921. Renewal 1949 by Wm. E. Booth-Clibborn. Assigned to ZHMI. All rights reserved. Used by permission.

Our modern songs often keep both of these central gospel facts in mind. Turn to Revelation 4 and rehear the two great songs to the Creator. Now go quickly to chapter 5 for the four great hymns to the Redeemer. Do you not see the similarity to a song like Stuart K. Hine's "How Great Thou Art"? The first stanza rings:

> O Lord my God! When I in awesome wonder
> Consider all the worlds Thy hands have made,
> I see the stars, I hear the rolling thunder,
> Thy pow'r throughout the universe displayed,
> Then sings my soul, my Savior God to Thee;
> How great Thou art, how great Thou art!

Yet, since you cannot stop at creation and you must go on to redemption, a further stanza adds:

> And when I think that God, His Son not sparing,
> Sent Him to die, I scarce can take it in;
> That on the cross my burden gladly bearing,
> He bled and died to take away my sin;
> Then sings my soul, my Savior God to thee;
> How great Thou art, how great Thou art![2]

The resurrection that followed the crucifixion is the event that established for all time that Jesus is the Son of God, and that the Father had accepted the Son's sacrifice. That resurrection incident lies behind the church's worshiping of Jesus Christ. The apostles were convinced that in Jesus the transcendent had become immanent, the afar-off had come near, the eternal had entered into time. Paul wrote, "God was in Christ reconciling the world unto himself" (2 Corinthians 5:19). The church believes that the death of Christ on Calvary took away our sins, and the resurrection from the garden grave gives us hope of everlasting life. If Jesus were less than God, then Revelation would make no sense and Christian worship would make no sense. Christians are monotheists and yet the monotheist John would fall at the feet of Jesus and invite everyone else in Heaven and earth to join him.

The Core of Worship

As we study Revelation to find how the early church worshiped, what have we learned thus far? We have found that the OBJECT *of worship* is our Lord and the BASIS *of that worship* is the gospel of Jesus dying and rising again. Thus, as sacrificed Lamb and reigning Lion, He is worthy. What we now seek is the CORE *of the early worship service.* It should not be hard to find. John is receiving his Patmos vision on the Lord's Day, the day of Christian worship. Modern liturgists and scholars say that we find in the book before us how the early church of Asia in A.D. 96 was worshiping. Christians were gathering on a certain day and acting in a certain way.

What is different about worship in a Christian church and that in a Jewish synagogue? There are some elements in Christian worship like you would find in any synagogue. In the synagogue they have prayer. You find prayer in a Christian assembly. Jews have Scripture reading. Christ's followers have Scripture reading when they meet. There are benedictions and calls to worship in both places of worship. But there are two distinctive elements in Christian worship: Sunday and the Supper. When the church gathered in John's day, there was a sacred day and a sacred dinner. There was a holy time and a holy table. There was the setting of the Lord's Day and there was the gem of the Lord's Supper. "Lord's" in the Greek is *kuriakos.* This adjective is used only twice in the New Testament. Once it is *kuriake heṁera,* the "Lord's day" (Revelation 1:10). The other time it is *kuriakon deipnon,* the "Lord's supper" (1 Corinthians 11:20). These two items are inseparably bound together in the book before us and show how early churchmen were worshiping. They met on the Lord's Day. They observed the Lord's Supper.

The only chronological date to which the book of Revelation calls our attention is *the day.* It does not tell what year it is because that is not important. It tells neither what month nor what day of the month it is, for that too is not significant. But it does tell you it is "the Lord's Day." John wants you to know what is that one day upon which he is most lonesome on this Isle of Patmos—the day that the Aegean Sea so noticeably separates him from his friends in Asia Minor. The day of key importance to him is "the Lord's Day." He would like to be with his church in gathered worship.

All of the visions of the book of Revelation come to John on that Lord's Day. John knows that after they are written down and delivered to the seven congregations of Asia Minor, there will not be individual copies for each believer. Rather, the people will hear the letter read to their assembly on another Lord's Day. The phrase "Lord's Day" is meant to be a liturgical suggestion.

Domitian and earlier emperors every week had an "Emperor's Day." Christians will have a "Lord's Day." It will not be just the Jewish Sabbath postponed for one day. It will be far more than this. It will be a new day with new meaning and it must have a new name. Hence, the name "Lord's Day" is given. A quick check with the *Didache,* with Ignatius of Antioch, with Justin Martyr and other church writings of the early centuries will show that "Lord's Day" is a title that always refers to the day we call Sunday.

In the Gospels (Matthew, Mark, Luke, and John) the day an event happened seldom is significant, for the exception of arguments between Jesus and the Pharisees over the Sabbath. You do not have it said that something occurred on the third day of the week or on the fifth or sixth day of the week. But Matthew, Mark, Luke, and John each say that when Christ rose, it was "the first day." These Gospel writers want you to understand the cause for Lord's Day worship. Why has the church, since Pentecost, been meeting upon "the first day of the week" for the breaking of bread (Acts 20:7)? Why did the saints in Galatia and Greece gather their benevolent offerings on "the first day of the week" (1 Corinthians 16:1, 2)? It is because this was the day Christ was proven to be Lord. This is the day when He often would appear to His disciples during the forty days that preceded His ascension.

The historic reason for the weekly eucharist was not simply the institution of the Supper on Thursday night of Christ's last week. Nor was it the "expectation of the Messianic Banquet," as Albert Schweitzer says. It rather seems to be the after-resurrection appearances of Christ when He would dine again with His followers, that is the explanation for this weekly meeting for the Lord's Supper. To this day, disciples gather to break bread anew with this living Christ. The Supper is held on the day of resurrection. A worshiper had his momentary backward glance to Christ's appearances. But he also had his anticipation of the end of time. The Lord's Supper was a foreshadow of the Bridal Banquet, the Messianic Feast. To this very hour disciples meet on the Lord's Day when, besides remembering the past, they anticipate "the day of the Lord." It should be stated also that the Communion table is a family table. Communing is not something to be done in private. Christians in the first centuries often were endangering their lives when they assembled on "the first day of the week" in time of persecution. Even then believers were not having the Lord's Supper in individual privacy. This was a family meal, the family of God gathered together.

There is no place for individualism, no place for sectarianism, no place for denominational thinking in the mind of John the Revelator. He is alone on Patmos, but he is conscious of the church everywhere. John is mentally with more than the church in Ephesus and Asia. He is thinking of the church in all lands plus Heaven above. John is contemplating the church now and hereafter, the church here and there, the church militant and triumphant.

I want us to sense the feeling of Greek Orthodox worship. The Western Church, both in its Anglican and its Roman parts, has lost this. The Roman church emphasizes the passion of Jesus. The Greek church emphasizes the resurrection, the victory, the presence of Jesus. The Orthodox have a screen called the *iconostasis* which represents the separation between earth and Heaven. Much of the liturgical action is going on behind this screen. Worshipers are aware that Heaven and earth are acting together in celebrating the victory of the Lamb. All members of God's family ought to feel this hopeful joy every time they come around the Lord's Table.

How does the book of Revelation end? Chapter 22 in the next-to-the-last verse reads, *maranatha,* that is "Our Lord, come." When John and Paul wrote letters to a church, they knew that the Lord's Supper concluded the worship. They also knew that Scriptures were read before the Communion. Along with the reading of the Old Testament, possibly would be the reading of some word from an apostle. It is for this reason that the letters often end with the anticipation of the Lord coming. It is not a coming at the end of the age alone. It is His coming, even momentarily, at the Lord's Table. "Our Lord, come."

Christianity is different from paganism. In paganism the temple is primarily to house the god, never to house the congregation. The important thing in pagan worship is the place, not the people. But in Judaism and Christianity, the religions of revelation, a building may be built, but it is the place of assembly so the family can get together.

Revelation 22:17 may be more than an invitation for non-Christians to come to Christ. It also may be a call for Christ to come to the church's Table. The more I look at the context the more I am driven to decide that this is a possible meaning. The verses before Revelation 22:17, and the verses following, talk about the coming Christ (even so "come Lord Jesus"). So the *Spirit,* who inspires John the prophet, says "Come." And the *Bride,* the church universal—responds, "Come." And *he who hears* the lector, who is reading the letter, joins in and says, "Come" to Jesus. There may be those just visiting the worship service who are not Christian, so the added phrase is given for the thirsty to come also to take of the water of life freely. It is God's desire for the ever-expanding circle of worshipers (including the living creatures, the twenty-four elders, and the multitude of angels) to keep reaching people from more tribes, nations, and tongues. Heaven's hope is for myriads more to come and bow the knee to Jesus Christ. The family of God ever is to expand.

The Goal of Worship

Revelation tells us the object of worship in the early time, and in every time, ought only to be the *Lord.* It tells us the reason for this is that *Jesus died and rose again.* These facts constitute the gospel. And even though Christians, like Jews and Muslims, pray and read Scripture, we have something distinctive and unique in the church. We have a *sacred Table and a sacred time.* These together tell the story of the gospel by drama. But we must yet inquire as to the desired end of that worship. Why does God call us to gather Sunday after Sunday to break the bread? God wants a response from us when we think about Calvary and the open tomb. The RESPONSE He wants is *first repentance and then praise.*

I am going to assume that you know Revelation. You know that of the seven churches, five are told to repent and to do their first works. Only the overcomer is promised a place in God's future. Only the overcomer will be given the white stone. He who does not repent will be given the black stone by this world's judge. Some will be redeemed forever. Others will be "blackballed" and damned forever.

In the dialogue and antiphonal worship of this book we have heard John speak, angels speak, living creatures speak, twenty-four elders speak, and choirs sing. We have seen virtues and vices held up before us. We have had pass before our eyes both the eternal city—the new Jerusalem—and the lake of fire filled with brimstone. Every reader is made aware that he had better examine himself. He knows that if he does not repent he is going to perish. First of all he needs to bow down and cry out for forgiveness. But he knows that next he is to stand tall and join his voice in God's praise.

In Luke 15, when a lost sheep is found, a lost coin is recovered, and a lost boy returns to his father's house, there is "music and dancing." So in Revelation, there is a central note of joy and praise. Handel's *Messiah* was written in 1741 in twenty-four days and was intended to cover, in three parts, the "Promise of the Incarnation," the "Passion Story," and the "Conquest of Death." George Frederick Handel was inspired by the words of doxology in Revelation 5:9-14, Revelation 11:15, and especially Revelation 19 for his great "Hallelujah Chorus." The custom has risen that when this chorus is sung in praise to God for His grace, everyone in the audience rises to his feet.

The reader of Revelation, who at first is drawn to his knees in awareness of sin, is called to his tallest stature in awareness of God's marvelous grace. Shall we with angels, elders, living creatures, and all the redeemed, sing, "All hail the power of Jesus' name" and with the "angels prostrate fall"? Shall we "bring forth the royal diadem and crown Him Lord of all"?

It is Biblical to say, "Amen!" It is right to cry, "Hallelujah!" It is Christian to shout, "Maranatha!" It is the nature of worship longingly to echo, "Our Lord, come!"

As we close this exceptional book of Revelation, we hope

never to forget three facts. It is revealed in Revelation that we are at WAR and the battle will rage until the last enemy is defeated. It is revealed that the Church's WORK will go on until the last soul is won. It is revealed that the WORSHIP of God and His Christ will continue until time is no more and then will not end as eternal ages roll.